A. James, S. Conrad, W. Hasselbrir

Engineering Federated Inf(

Proceedings of the 5th Workshop EFIS 2003
July 17–18, 2003
Coventry (UK)

Volume Editors:

Dr. Anne James
Data and Knowledge Engineering Research Group (DKERG)
School of Mathematical and Information Sciences
Coventry University
Coventry, CV15FB, UK

Prof. Dr. Stefan Conrad
Heinrich-Heine-Universität Düsseldorf
Institut für Informatik (Computer Science)
Universitätsstr. 1
D-40225 Düsseldorf, Germany

Prof. Dr. Wilhelm Hasselbring
Universität Oldenburg
Informatik / Software Engineering
Postfach 2503
D-26111 Oldenburg, Germany

Bibliographic information published by Die Deutsche Bibliothek
Die Deutsche Bibliothek lists this publication in the Deutsche Nationalbibliografie;
detailed bibligraphic data is availalable in the Internet at http://dnb.ddb.de.

© 2003 Akademische Verlagsgesellschaft Aka GmbH, Berlin

"infix" is a joint imprint of Akademische Verlagsgesellschaft Aka GmbH (Berlin) and IOS
Press BV (Amsterdam)

Reproduced from electronic file supplied by the authors
Printing and Binding: Hundt Druck GmbH, Köln
Printed in Germany

ISBN 3-89838-041-6
ISBN 1-58603-359-X

Preface

Engineering of Federated Information Systems is a research area which addresses the systematic development of interoperation solutions for autonomous, heterogeneous systems covering both database and non-database information sources. As many examples of information systems in application areas such as business, finance, environmental science, and medicine show, there is an increasing need to make information available through some form of network (enterprise network or even the WWW), not only for "global" applications, but also for local applications using semantically related information.

EFIS 2003 is the fifth workshop in an international workshop series. Starting in 1997 a workshop on Engineering Federated Databases Systems (EFDBS) was held in Barcelona. Taking into account that databases are only one important part in typical integration projects the title of the wokshop was then extended to Engineering Federated Information Systems (EFIS), thus covering more aspects in the area of informaton systems integration. The next EFIS workshops were held in Kühlungsborn (1999), Dublin (2000), and Berlin (2001). Reports stressing the research topics identified in the discussion on these workshops can be found in ACM SIGMOD Records 26(4), Dec. 1997, 28(3), Sept. 1999, and 29(4), Dec. 2000 as well as in The Computer Journal 45(2), 2002.

More detailed information on previous workshops in this series is available on http://www.informatik.uni-trier.de/~ley/db/conf/efdbs/.

An international program committee reviewed all submissions and finally selected 12 papers (9 as long papers and 3 as position or short papers). We are grateful to the members of the program committee and to the additional reviewers involved. Furthermore, we want to express our thanks to Rachel Carter, Serena Morgan and Muhammed Younas of the organising team at Coventry University.

Coventry, July 2003   Anne James
                                                          Stefan Conrad
                                                          Wilhelm Hasselbring

Program Committee:

S. Conrad (University of Düsseldorf, Germany) (co-chair)

B. Eaglestone (University of Sheffield, UK)

A. Gray (University of Wales, UK)

J. Grimson (Trinity College, Ireland)

W. Hasselbring (University of Oldenburg, Germany) (co-chair)

A. Heuer (University of Rostock, Germany)

W.-J. van den Heuvel (Tilburg University, The Netherlands)

A. James (Coventry University, UK) (co-chair)

M. Klettke (University of Rostock, Germany)

R.-D. Kutsche (Technical University Berlin, Germany)

A. Poulovassilis (Birkbeck College, UK)

M. Roantree (Dublin City University, Ireland)

G. Saake (University of Magdeburg, Germany)

F. Saltor (Universitat Politecnica de Catalunya, Catalonia)

K. Subieta (Institute of Computer Science, Poland)

Y. Yang (Swinburne University of Technology, Australia)

Additional Reviewers:

H. Niemann (University of Oldenburg, Germany)

Ch. Popfinger (University of Düsseldorf, Germany)

K.-U. Sattler (University of Magdeburg,Germany)

C. Türker (ETH Zurich, Switzerland)

Local Organisers:

Anne James (Coventry University, UK)

Muhammed Younas (Coventry University, UK)

Table of Contents

Invited Talks

Regular Papers

What is Interesting about Scientific Databases?

Peter Buneman

University of Edinburgh

Abstract

Much of modern scientific research depends on databases, but do we need anything more than conventional database technology to support scientific data?
If you listen to physicists, the main problem is the size of the databases – the
petabytes of data that will gush from their accelerators in the next few years.
Now size matters (at least physicists worry about it) but there are other issues,
important to scientfic data, that have received little attention from database
research. In this talk I want raise some of them:

Annotation of existing data now provides a new form of communication between scientists, but conventional database technology provides little support
for attaching annotations. I shall show why new models of both data and query
languages are needed.

Closely related to annotation is provenance – knowing where your data has
come from. This is now a real problem in bioinformatics with literally hundreds of
databases, most of which are derived from others by a process of transformation,
correction and annotation.

Preserving past states of a database – archiving – is also important for veri-
fying the basis of scientific research, yet few published scientific databases do a
good job of archiving. Past "editions" of the database get lost. I shall describe
a system that allows frequent archiving and efficient retrieval with remarkably
little space overhead.

Finally does the fact that updates in scientific data are relatively infrequent
allow us to use different storage models? I shall suggest that it enables us to
resurrect an old idea of "vertical partitioning" that is both effective and helps
to unify database and scientific programming.

GRIDs and Ambient Computing: The Next Generation

Keith G Jeffery

Director, Information Technology, CLRC-Rutherford Appleton Laboratory Chilton, Didcot, Oxfordshire, UK

Abstract. This paper describes a new IT (Information Technology) architecture which has the potential to revolutionise the way we work and live. GRIDs provides facilities for integrating heterogeneous data sources or for data exchange between different sources to provide information. It provides knowledge discovery in databases capability using data mining techniques. It provides metacomputing and thus access to massive computational resources. It permits integration of information and computation, of new data collection and appropriate user interface in a 'deal' for the end-user. The whole system is protected against misuse by authentication and authorisation subsystems. When Ambient computing techniques are used to access a GRIDs system then the end-user has access anytime, anyhow, anywhere.

1 Introduction

We live in a complex and fast-changing world. There is a tidal wave of data from sensors and video cameras. The requirements of business, travel, agriculture, production industry, mineral extraction, pharmaceuticals and other commercial activities all require information and knowledge to be extracted from these vast volumes of data in such a way as to assist human decision-making. Leisure activities such as tourism, culture, entertainment require similar facilities. Furthermore, the end-users require presentation to be correct and in the appropriate form, at the right place in a timely fashion.

The overall requirement is to collect data which represents accurately the real world, and then to process it to information (structured data in context) from which can be extracted knowledge (justified commonly held belief). This, together with a cooperative working environment, provides the capability for decision support and problem solving. It also provides an environment for enjoyment of culture and education. The next generation GRIDs technology combined with Ambient Computing meets the need.

Since proposing the idea described here formally in 1999, the author and his team have been actively researching the area. It combines well with our work managing the UK and Ireland Office of W3C (the World Wide Web Consortium) and associated work on standards.

2 The Problem

Present-day systems are heterogeneous and poorly interlinked. Humans have to search for information from many sources and find it stored in different character sets, languages, data formats. It may be stored in different measurement units, at different precision, with different accuracies more-or-less supported by calibration data. Worse, having found appropriate sources they have to find sufficient computing power to process the data, to integrate it together to a useful form for the problem at hand and suitable visualisation capabilities to provide a human-understandable view of the information. Suitable expert decision support systems and data mining tools for the creation of knowledge from information, and communications environments for group decision-making, are also hard to find and use. Behind all this is the need for accurate (represents accurately the world of interest) and precise (measured correctly) data; this requires appropriate data collection devices, supporting software and validation systems. The new paradigms of GRIDs and Ambient Computing are an attempt to overcome these problems.

The paper is organised as follows: in section 3 the GRIDs concept is described. The architecture is detailed in Section 4. Ambient Computing described in Section 5. Then in Section 6 the research issues are explored.

3 GRIDs

The Idea In 1998-1999 the UK Research Council community was proposing future programmes for R&D. The author was asked to propose an integrating IT architecture. The proposal was based on concepts including distributed computing, metacomputing, metadata, middleware, client-server migrating to three-layer architectures and knowledge-based assists. The novelty lay in the integration of various techniques into one architectural framework.

The Requirement The UK Research Council community of researchers was facing several IT-based problems. Their ambitions for scientific discovery included post-genomic discoveries, climate change understanding, oceanographic studies, environmental pollution monitoring and modelling, precise materials science, studies of combustion processes, advanced engineering, pharmaceutical design, and particle physics data handling and simulation. They needed more processor power, more data storage capacity, better analysis and visualisation — all supported by easy-to-use tools controlled through an intuitive user interface.

Architecture Overview The architecture proposed consists of three layers (Figure 1). The computation / data grid has supercomputers, large servers, massive data storage facilities and specialised devices and facilities (e.g. for VR (Virtual Reality)) all linked by high-speed networking and forms the lowest layer. The main functions include compute load sharing / algorithm partitioning, resolution of data source addresses, security, replication and message rerouting. The

3

information grid is superimposed on the computation / data grid and resolves homogeneous access to heterogeneous information sources mainly through the use of metadata and middleware. Finally, the uppermost layer is the knowledge grid which utilises knowledge discovery in database technology to generate knowledge and also allows for representation of knowledge through scholarly works, peer-reviewed (publications) and grey literature, the latter especially hyperlinked to information and data to sustain the assertions in the knowledge.

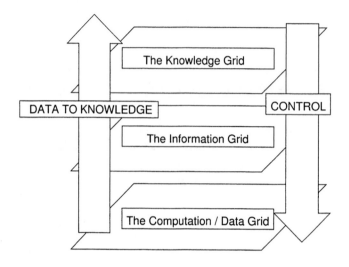

Fig. 1. The 3-Layer GRIDs Architecture

The concept is based on the idea of a uniform landscape within the GRIDs domain, the complexity of which is masked by easy-to-use interfaces. To this facility are connected external appliances — ranging from supercomputers, storage access networks, data storage robots, specialised visualisation and VR systems, data sensors and detectors (e.g. on satellites) to user client devices such as workstations and PDAs (Personal Digital Assistants). The connection between the external appliances and the GRIDs domain is through agents, supported by metadata, representing the appliance (and thus continuously available to the GRIDs systems). These representative agents handle credentials of the end-user in their current role, appliance characteristics and interaction preferences (for both user client appliances and service appliances), preference profiles and associated organisational information. These agents interact with other agents in the usual way via brokers to locate services and negotiate use. The key aspect is that all the agent interaction is based upon available metadata.

The GRID In 1998 — in parallel with the initial UK thinking on GRIDs — Ian Foster and Carl Kesselman published a collection of papers in a book generally known as 'The GRID Bible' [1]. The essential idea is to connect together super-computers to provide more power — the metacomputing technique. However, the major contribution lies in the systems and protocols for compute resource scheduling. Additionally, the designers of the GRID realised that these linked supercomputers would need fast data feeds so developed GRIDFTP. Finally, basic systems for authentication and authorisation are described. The GRID has encompassed the use of SRB (Storage Request Broker) from SDSC (San Diego Supercomputer Centre) for massive data handling. SRB has its propri-etary metadata system to assist in locating relevant data resources. It also uses LDAP as its directory of resources.

The GRID corresponds to the lowest grid layer (computation / data layer) of the GRIDs architecture.

4 The GRIDs Architecture

4.1 Introduction

The idea behind GRIDs is to provide an IT environment that interacts with the user to determine the user requirement for service and then satisfies that re-quirement across a heterogeneous environment of data stores, processing power, special facilities for display and data collection systems thus making the IT en-vironment appear homogeneous to the end-user.

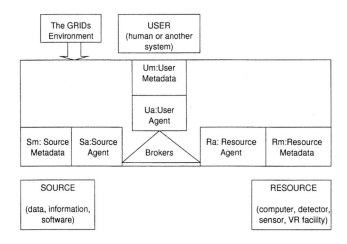

Fig. 2. The GRIDs Components

Referring to Fig. 2, the major components external to the GRIDs environ-ment are:

a) users: each being a human or another system;

b) sources: data, information or software
c) resources: such as computers, sensors, detectors, visualisation or VR (virtual reality) facilities

Each of these three major components is represented continuously and actively within the GRIDs environment by:

1) metadata: which describes the external component and which is changed with changes in circumstances through events
2) an agent: which acts on behalf of the external resource representing it within the GRIDs environment.

As a simple example, the agent could be regarded as the answering service of a person's mobile phone and the metadata as the instructions given to the service such as 'divert to service when busy' and / or 'divert to service if unanswered'.

Finally there is a component which acts as a 'go between' between the agents. These are brokers which, as software components, act much in the same way as human brokers by arranging agreements and deals between agents, by acting themselves (or using other agents) to locate sources and resources, to manage data integration, to ensure authentication of external components and authorisation of rights to use by an authenticated component and to monitor the overall system.

From this it is clear that they key components are the metadata, the agents and the brokers.

Metadata Metadata is data about data [2]. An example might be a product tag attached to a product (e.g. a tag attached to a piece of clothing) that is available for sale. The metadata on the product tag tells the end-user (human considering purchasing the article of clothing) data about the article itself — such as the fibres from which it is made, the way it should be cleaned, its size (possibly in different classification schemes such as European, British, American) and maybe style, designer and other useful data. The metadata tag may be attached directly to the garment, or it may appear in a catalogue of clothing articles offered for sale (or, more usually, both). The metadata may be used to make a selection of potentially interesting articles of clothing before the actual articles are inspected, thus improving convenience. Today this concept is widely-used. Much e-commerce is based on B2C (Business to Customer) transactions based on an online catalogue (metadata) of goods offered. One well-known example is www.amazon.com.

What is metadata to one application may be data to another. For example, an electronic library catalogue card is metadata to a person searching for a book on a particular topic, but data to the catalogue system of the library which will be grouping books in various ways: by author, classification code, shelf position, title — depending on the purpose required.

It is increasingly accepted that there are several kinds of metadata. The classification proposed (Fig. 3) is gaining wide acceptance and is detailed below.

6

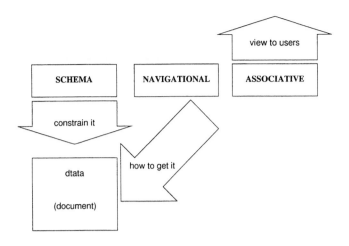

Fig. 3. Metadata Classification

Schema Metadata Schema metadata constrains the associated data. It defines the intension whereas instances of data are the extension. From the intension a theoretical universal extension can be created, constrained only by the intension. Conversely, any observed instance should be a subset of the theoretical extension and should obey the constraints defined in the intension (schema). One problem with existing schema metadata (e.g. schemas for relational DBMS) is that they lack certain intensional information that is required [3]. Systems for information retrieval based on, e.g. the SGML (Standard Generalised Markup Language) DTD (Document Type Definition) experience similar problems.

It is noticeable that many ad hoc systems for data exchange between systems send with the data instances a schema that is richer than that in conventional DBMS — to assist the software (and people) handling the exchange to utilise the exchanged data to best advantage.

Navigational Metadata Navigational metadata provides the pathway or routing to the data described by the schema metadata or associative metadata. In the RDF model it is a URL (universal resource locator), or more accurately, a URI (Universal Resource Identifier). With increasing use of databases to store resources, the most common navigational metadata now is a URL with associated query parameters embedded in the string to be used by CGI (Common Gateway Interface) software or proprietary software for a particular DBMS product or DBMS-Webserver software pairing.

The navigational metadata describes only the physical access path. Naturally, associated with a particular URI are other properties such as:

a) security and privacy (e.g. a password required to access the target of the URI);

b) access rights and charges (e.g. does one have to pay to access the resource at the URI target);

c) constraints over traversing the hyperlink mapped by the URI (e.g. the target of the URI is only available if previously a field on a form has been input with a value between 10 and 20). Another example would be the hypermedia equivalent of referential integrity in a relational database;

d) semantics describing the hyperlink such as 'the target resource describes the son of the person described in the origin resource'

However, these properties are best described by associative metadata which then allows more convenient co-processing in context of metadata describing both resources and hyperlinks between them and — if appropriate — events.

Associative Metadata In the data and information domain associative metadata can describe:

a) a set of data (e.g. a database, a relation (table) or a collection of documents or a retrieved subset). An example would be a description of a dataset collected as part of a scientific mission;

b) an individual instance (record, tuple, document). An example would be a library catalogue record describing a book;

c) an attribute (column in a table, field in a set of records, named element in a set of documents). An example would be the accuracy / precision of instances of the attribute in a particular scientific experiment;

d) domain information (e.g. value range) of an attribute. An example would be the range of acceptable values in a numeric field such as the capacity of a car engine or the list of valid values in an enumerated list such as the list of names of car manufacturers;

e) a record / field intersection unique value (i.e. value of one attribute in one instance) This would be used to explain an apparently anomalous value.

In the relationship domain, associative metadata can describe relationships between sets of data e.g. hyperlinks. Associative metadata can — with more flexibility and expressivity than available in e.g. relational database technology or hypermedia document system technology — describe the semantics of a relationship, the constraints, the roles of the entities (objects) involved and additional constraints.

In the process domain, associative metadata can describe (among other things) the functionality of the process, its external interface characteristics, restrictions on utilisation of the process and its performance requirements / characteristics.

In the event domain, associative metadata can describe the event, the temporal constraints associated with it, the other constraints associated with it and actions arising from the event occurring.

Associative metadata can also be personalised: given clear relationships between them that can be resolved automatically and unambiguously, different metadata describing the same base data may be used by different users.

8

Taking an orthogonal view over these different kinds of information system objects to be described, associative metadata may be classified as follows:

1) descriptive: provides additional information about the object to assist in understanding and using it;
2) restrictive: provides additional information about the object to restrict access to authorised users and is related to security, privacy, access rights, copyright and IPR (Intellectual Property Rights);
3) supportive: a separate and general information resource that can be cross-linked to an individual object to provide additional information e.g. translation to a different language, super- or sub-terms to improve a query — the kind of support provided by a thesaurus or domain ontology;

Most examples of metadata in use today include some components of most of these kinds but neither structured formally nor specified formally so that the metadata tends to be of limited use for automated operations — particularly interoperation — thus requiring additional human interpretation.

4.2 Agents

Agents operate continuously and autonomously and act on behalf of the external component they represent. They interact with other agents via brokers, whose task it is to locate suitable agents for the requested purpose. An agent's actions are controlled to a large extent by the associated metadata which should include either instructions, or constraints, such that the agent can act directly or deduce what action is to be taken. Each agent is waiting to be 'woken up' by some kind of event; on receipt of a message the agent interprets the message and — using the metadata as parametric control — executes the appropriate action, either communicating with the external component (user, source or resource) or with brokers as a conduit to other agents representing other external components.

An agent representing an end-user accepts a request from the end-user and interacts with the end-user to refine the request (clarification and precision), first based on the user metadata and then based on the results of a first attempt to locate (via brokers and other agents) appropriate sources and resources to satisfy the request. The proposed activity within GRIDs for that request is presented to the end-user as a 'deal' with any costs, restrictions on rights of use etc. Assuming the user accepts the offered deal, the GRIDs environment then satisfies it using appropriate resources and sources and finally sends the result back to the user agent where — again using metadata — end-user presentation is determined and executed.

An agent representing a source will — with the associated metadata — respond to requests (via brokers) from other agents concerning the data or information stored, or the properties of the software stored. Assuming the deal with the end-user is accepted, the agent performs the retrieval of data requested, or supply of software requested.

An agent representing a resource — with the associated metadata — responds to requests for utilisation of the resource with details of any costs, restrictions and relevant capabilities. Assuming the deal with the end-user is accepted the resource agent then schedules its contribution to providing the result to the end-user.

4.3   Brokers

Brokers act as 'go betweens' between agents. Their task is to accept messages from an agent which request some external component (source, resource or user), identify an external component that can satisfy the request by its agent working with its associated metadata and either put the two agents in direct contact or continue to act as an intermediary, possibly invoking other brokers (and possibly agents) to handle, for example, measurement unit conversion or textual word translation.

Other brokers perform system monitoring functions including overseeing performance (and if necessary requesting more resources to contribute to the overall system e.g. more networking bandwidth or more compute power). They may also monitor usage of external components both for statistical purposes and possibly for any charging scheme.

4.4   The Components Working Together

Now let us consider how the components interact. An agent representing a user may request a broker to find an agent representing another external component such as a source or a resource. The broker will usually consult a directory service (itself controlled by an agent) to locate potential agents representing suitable sources or resources. The information will be returned to the requesting (user) agent, probably with recommendations as to order of preference based on criteria concerning the offered services. The user agent matches these against preferences expressed in the metadata associated with the user and makes a choice. The user agent then makes the appropriate recommendation to the end-user who in turn decides to 'accept the deal' or not.

5   Ambient Computing

The concept of ambient computing implies that the computing environment is always present and available in an even manner. The concept of pervasive computing implies that the computing environment is available everywhere and is 'into everything'. The concept of mobile computing implies that the end-user device may be connected even when on the move. In general usage of the term, ambient computing implies both pervasive and mobile computing.

The idea, then, is that an end-user may find herself connected (or connectable — she may choose to be disconnected) to the computing environment all the time. The computing environment may involve information provision (access to database and web facilities), office functions (calendar, email, directory), desktop functions (word processing, spreadsheet, presentation editor), perhaps project management software and systems specialised for her application needs — accessed from her end-user device connected back to 'home base' so that her view of the world is as if at her desk. In addition entertainment subsystems (video, audio, games) should be available.

A typical configuration might comprise:

a) a headset with earphone(s) and microphone for audio communication, connected by bluetooth wireless local connection to

b) a PDA (personal digital assistant) with small screen, numeric/text keyboard (like a telephone), GSM/GPRS (mobile phone) connections for voice and data, wireless LAN connectivity and ports for connecting sensor devices (to measure anything close to the end-user) in turn connected by bluetooth to

c) an optional notebook computer carried in a backpack (but taken out for use in a suitable environment) with conventional screen, keyboard, large hard disk and connectivity through GSM/GPRS, wireless LAN, cable LAN and dial-up telephone

The end-user would perhaps use only (a) and (b) (or maybe (b) alone using the built in speaker and microphone) in a social or professional context as mobile phone and 'filofax', and as entertainment centre, with or without connectivity to 'home base' servers and IT environment. For more traditional working requiring keyboard and screen the notebook computer would be used, probably without the PDA. The two might be used together with data collection validation / calibration software on the notebook computer and sensors attached to the PDA.

The balance between that (data, software) which is on servers accessed over the network and that which is on (one of) the end-user device(s) depends on the mode of work, speed of required response and likelihood of interrupted connections. Clearly the GRIDs environment is ideal for such a user to be connected.

Such a configuration is clearly useful for a 'road warrior' (travelling salesman), for emergency services such as firefighters or paramedics, for businessmen, for production industry managers, for the distribution / logistics industry (warehousing, transport, delivery), for scientists in the field. and also for leisure activities such as mountain walking, visiting an art gallery, locating a restaurant or visiting an archaeological site.

6   Research Issues

Such an IT architectural environment inevitably poses challenging research issues. The major ones are:

Metadata Since metadata is critically important for interoperation and semantic understanding, there is a requirement for precise and formal representation of metadata to allow automated processing. Research is required into the metadata representation language expressivity in order to represent the entities user, source, resource. For example, the existing Dublin Core Metadata standard [4] is machine-readable but not machine-understandable, and furthermore mixes navigational, associative descriptive and associative restrictive metadata. A formal version has been proposed [5].

Agents There is an interesting research area concerning the generality or specificity of agents. Agents could be specialised for a particular task or generalised and configured dynamically for the task by metadata. Furthermore, agents may well need to be reactive and dynamically reconfigured by events / messages. This would cause a designer to lean towards general agents with dynamic configuration, but there are performance, reliability and security issues. In addition there are research issues concerning the syntax and semantics of messages passed between agents and brokers to ensure optimal representation with appropriate performance and security.

Brokers A similar research question is posed for brokers — are they generalised and dynamic or specific? However, brokers have not just representational functions, they have also to negotiate. The degree of autonomy becomes the key research issue: can the broker decide by itself or does it solicit input from the external entity (user, source, resource) via its agent and metadata? The broker will need general strategic knowledge (negotiation techniques) but the way a broker uses the additional information supplied by the agents representing the entities could be a differentiating factor and therefore a potential business benefit. In addition there are research issues concerning the syntax and semantics of messages passed between brokers to ensure optimal representation with appropriate performance and security.

Security Security is an issue in any system, and particularly in a distributed system. It becomes even more important if the system is a common marketplace with great heterogeneity of purpose and intent. The security takes the forms:

a) prevention of unauthorised access: this requires authentication of the user, authorisation of the user to access or use a source or resource and provision or denial of that access. The current heterogeneity of authentication and authorisation mechanisms provides many opportunities for deliberate or unwitting security exposure;

b) ensuring availability of the source or resource: this requires techniques such as replication, mirroring and hot or warm failover. There are deep research issues in transactions and rollback/recovery and optimisation;

c) ensuring continuity of service: this relates to (b) but includes additional fallback procedures and facilities and there are research issues concerning the optimal (cost-effective) assurance of continuity. In the case of interrupted communication there is a requirement for synchronisation of the end-user's view of the system between that which is required on the PDA and / or laptop and the servers.

There are particular problems with wireless communications because of interception. Encryption of sensitive transmissions is available but there remain research issues concerning security assurance.

Privacy The privacy issues concern essentially the tradeoff of personal information provision for intelligent system reaction. There are research issues on the optimal balance for particular end-user requirements. Furthermore, data protection legislation in countries varies and there are research issues concerning the requirement to provide data or to conceal data.

Trust When any end-user purchases online (e.g. a book from www.amazon.com) there is a trust that the supplier will deliver the goods and that the purchaser's credit card information is valid. This concept requires much extension in the case of contracts for supply of engineered components for assembly into e.g. a car. The provision of an e-marketplace brings with it the need for e-tendering, e-contracts, e-payments, e-guarantees as well s opportunities to re-engineer the business process for effectiveness and efficiency. This is currently a very hot research topic since it requires the representation in an IT system of artefacts (documents) associated with business transactions.

7 Conclusion

The GRIDs architecture will provide an IT infrastructure to revolutionise and expedite the way in which we do business and achieve leisure. The Ambient Computing architecture will revolutionise the way in which the IT infrastructure intersects with our lives, both professional and social. The two architectures in combination will provide the springboard for the greatest advances yet in Information Technology.

References

1. I Foster and C Kesselman (Eds). The Grid: Blueprint for a New Computing Infrastructure. Morgan-Kauffman 1998
2. K G Jeffery. 'Metadata': in Brinkkemper,J; Lindencrona,E; Solvberg,A: 'Information Systems Engineering' Springer Verlag, London 2000. ISBN 1-85233-317-0.
3. K G Jeffery, E K Hutchinson, J R Kalmus, M D Wilson, W Behrendt, C A Macnee, 'A Model for Heterogeneous Distributed Databases' Proceedings BNCOD12 July 1994; LNCS 826 pp 221-234 Springer-Verlag 1994
4. http://purl.oclc.org/dc/
5. Jeffery, K G: 'An Architecture for Grey Literature in a R&D Context' Proceedings GL'99 (Grey Literature) Conference Washington DC October 1999 http://www.konbib.nl/greynet/frame4.htm

Analyzing Uncertainties in the Database Integration Process by Means of Latent Class Analysis *

Evguenia Altareva and Stefan Conrad

Institute of Computer Science — Database Systems
Heinrich–Heine–University Düsseldorf
D–40225 Düsseldorf, Germany
{altareva|conrad}@cs.uni-duesseldorf.de

Abstract. We propose a methodological framework for building a statistical integration model for heterogeneous data sources.

We apply latent class analysis, a well-established statistical method, to investigate the relationships between entities in data sources as relationships among dependent variables, with the purpose of discovering the latent factors that affect them. The latent factors are associated with the real world entities which are unobservable in the sense that we do not know the real world class memberships, but only the stored data.

The approach provides an evaluation of uncertainties which aggregate in the integration process. The key parameter evaluated by the method is the real world class membership probability. Its value varies depending on the selection criteria applied in the pre-integration stages and in the subsequent integration steps. Therefore, we can evaluate various selection criteria and various integration strategies in order to optimize the integration process.

1 Introduction

There is a huge amount of data sources containing semantically related data that have been designed independently and for different purposes. They have different data models, data manipulating languages and, as consequence, have no common database management system. The task of integration, leading to effective and transparent accessibility of such data, exists in a number of application domains. It represents a difficult and complex problem, especially for heterogeneous and semi-structured data sources for which the structure and semantics are not completely known.

The integration process consists of consequently employing certain techniques in different stages of integration, as shown in figure 1.

* Part of this work has been supported by the German Science Foundation DFG (grant no. CO 207/13-1); project DIAsDEM: Data Integration for Legacy Systems and Semi-Structured Documents Employing Data Mining Techniques.

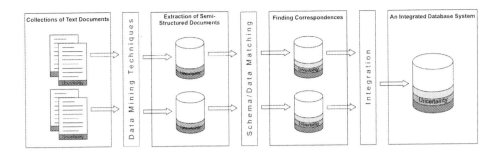

Fig. 1. The integration process

In the first step of integration we employ various data mining techniques for deriving structural properties, functional dependencies and class membership in each data source. The next step is to find correspondences between two input sources. In this step we use schema matching techniques to determine the correspondences on the schema level (structural correspondences). Then one has to define the correspondences between objects of two data sources. For this purpose numerous methods from the area of data cleaning could be used. Finally, after we have collected all the information about each source and about the correspondences between the sources, the schema integration and then data integration can be carried out.

In general the input data sources already contain uncertain information. The uncertainty increases with every integration step since every method contributes an additional uncertainty. These uncertainties can be expressed in terms of probability, support, confidence level, etc. The types of uncertainty can basically be classified with respect to their origins in the integration process as follows (cf. [1]):

⋄ uncertainty about the exact structure of data objects,
⋄ uncertainty concerning the assignment of data objects to classes,
⋄ uncertainty concerning the extensional correspondence between classes from two data sources.

The accumulation of uncertainties during the integration, when it is not controlled, may affect the final result in a crucial and unpredictable way. In [2] we examine some problems caused by the uncertainties occurring in the integration process.

In this paper we propose a framework for applying statistical analysis in order to take control over uncertainties and their propagation during the integration.

The remainder of this paper is organized as follows. We discuss related work in section 2. Then in section 3 we consider the problem of setting up a statistical model for the task of integration. The basic principles of latent variable models will be described in section 4. In section 5 we illustrate the application of latent class analysis by means of a simple integration example. In section 6 we give a brief summary and outlook.

2 Related Work

A major part of the bibliography on the integration of heterogeneous data sources is devoted to the specific problems of the integration process such as schema integration, schema matching, data cleaning, etc.

In [11], [12] various general techniques for *schema integration* are presented. These methods assume that the data to be integrated is exactly defined. Therefore, the application of these methods to data sources which contain a large fraction of uncertain information is problematic.

Various methods of *schema matching* (e.g. MOMIS [5], DIKE [9]) have been developed. A very detailed classification of matching techniques is given in [10]. The result of the schema matching procedure is the value of similarity between corresponding schema nodes. It also cannot be considered as an exact input knowledge for a subsequent schema integration.

For finding similarities between objects from different data sources *data cleaning* techniques [6], [8] should be applied. These techniques never deliver exact information about the similarities, but with a certain support.

On one hand, the heterogeneous semi-structured data which in principal contains uncertain information can only be integrated after applying the methods mentioned above. Therefore, the input for integration becomes even more uncertain. The uncertainties interact with each other and accumulate over the integration process.

On the other hand, the existing integration techniques require exact input information about the input sources and about the correspondences between them.

Thus, the analysis of uncertainties and their propagation in the integration process is a new task. For this task statistical analysis can be employed. We see numerous examples for applying statistical methods in the domain of knowledge discovery. For instance, the latent variable models, in particular factor analysis and principal component analysis, are successfully used in data mining for finding a structure and reducing dimensionality. For an overview and further references see [7].

In the integration domain the stated methods have not been employed yet. We see a challenge in developing a methodological framework which extends the application area of statistical methods to the integration domain.

3 Statistical Model of the Integration Task

We propose the analysis of the uncertainties and their propagation from one integration step to another using well-established statistical methods. Their application requires to build a statistical model of the integration task.

Generally, the integration of k data sources includes two major stages. At the first step we determine the correspondences of schema nodes of these data sources and build the integrated schema. At the next step the correspondences between the objects from corresponding schema nodes (class, subclass) are established.

Thus, for each schema node we have a set of n objects and a knowledge (partly uncertain) about their class membership. This information can be presented as a table of the class membership of objects in each data source, shown in figure 2. We denote the class membership with the following values.

$$x_{i,j} = \begin{cases} 0 \text{ missing data} \\ 1 \text{ if object belongs to the class} \\ 2 \text{ if object does not belong to the class} \end{cases}$$

Data Sources

i \ j	1	2	...	k	
1	1	1	...	1	
2	1	1	...	1	I
⋮	⋮	⋮	⋮	⋮	
⋮	1	1	...	1	
⋮	2	1	...	1	
⋮	1	1	...	2	II
⋮	⋮	⋮	⋮	⋮	
⋮	1	2	...	1	
⋮	1	0	...	1	
⋮	0	1	...	0	III
⋮	⋮	⋮	⋮	⋮	
n	1	1	...	0	

Objects

Fig. 2. Class membership table

where subscript $i = 1, 2, \ldots, k$ refers to the data source, $j = 1, 2, \ldots, n$ is the object number.

A set of values $x_{i,j}$ forms the $n \times k$ matrix of class membership X.

We do not assign a certain row to a certain object, but assume that the rows can be sorted in order to compose a clear structure of the table. We distinguish three different parts in the table, namely, the definite part (I) which includes the objects which are presented in each data source (equivalence), a so-called random part (II) which includes all the uncertainties, and a part (III) which includes missing data (disjoint).

The random part presents mistakes of two types, when the object belongs to the class but was defined as "2" and the object does not belong to the class being defined as "1". In ideal case, the random part should include the rows with the random combinations of "1" and "2", the rows with only "1" or only "2" are possible as well. Therefore, the random part cannot be mechanically separated from the other parts. A statistical method should be applied for this.

Thus this table is a collection of correct and random data. All three types of uncertainties described in [1] contribute to the values $x_{i,j}$.

The information we deal with has a discrete nature. Every real object is unique and cannot have a partial class membership. On contrary, the statistics does not make any difference between objects and considers a class membership of each object as a single measurement (or trial) of the random variable assigned to this class.

We construct the table based on the data obtained by various methods used in the integration process. In fact it is not possible to identify a certain object with a certain row. The table should be reconstructed using the integral parameters delivered by the applied techniques such as data mining, schema matching, data cleaning, etc.

The support of the objects' class membership for each data source is provided by data mining techniques. Therefore, the proportion of values "0", "1", "2" in every column of the class membership table is known.

Schema matching delivers the support of class correspondence. We use this information together with the information obtained by data mining and data cleaning to find the parts of the table which should be disjoint for every pair of data sources.

The value of integral parameter (for example, support of class membership) means that the corresponding column of the table contains a certain number of "1" and "2", but there is no information which row contains "1" and which row contains "2". Therefore, we can sort the values in every column in order to fit the value of the class correspondence support. This integral parameter is responsible for the relative number of combinations "1-2", "2-1", "1-1" and "2-2" for every two columns of the table.

This information may not be sufficient for the complete reconstruction of the class membership table, but this is not really needed for applying statistical methods.

In section 5 we describe how the statistical analysis evaluates various uncertainties. For this we consider a case when the first two columns of the table are assigned to two input data sources and the third column is reserved for the integrated database. The values in this column are of our choice, depending on the integration strategy for which the expert's decisions could be important. Therefore, there could be cases that objects belonging to the classes in the input data sources are not included into the integrated database and vice versa.

Below we describe the basic concepts of Latent Variable Models which we use for the statistical analysis.

4 Latent Variable Models

4.1 Principles of Latent Variable Models

Latent variable models provide an important tool for the analysis of multivariate data. They offer a conceptual framework within which many disparate methods can be unified and a base from which new methods can be developed. Latent variable models include such methods as factor analysis, clustering and multidimensional scaling, latent class analysis, latent trait analysis, latent profile analysis, etc. [3], [4].

Latent variable models are based on the statistical model and are used to study the patterns of relationship among many dependent variables, with the goal of discovering something about the nature of the latent (unobservable) variables that affect them, even through those latent variables were not measured directly. The latent variables are called factors. Dependent variables used in Latent Variable Models are manifest variables which can be directly observed.

In section 3 we have described the class membership table where the dependent variables are associated with data sources. The values of these variables present the objects' class membership. A latent variable corresponds to real world class membership. This membership is unobservable (in the sense that we only have the stored data at hand) and it does determine class membership in both input data sources and in an integrated database.

Generally, both latent and manifest variables could be metrical or categorical. Metrical variables have realized values in the set of real numbers and may be discrete or continuous. Categorical variables assign individuals to one of a set of categories.

The relevant method for the integration task is latent class analysis (LCA), since both latent and manifest variables are categorical.

LCA allows us to define which part of our sample is defined by the latent class and which part is a random part. This is equivalent to the decomposition of our sample matrix in two parts, where one part consists only of positive responses (defined by the latent class), and another, random part. There should not be any correlation between the variables for the random part. This is a restriction of the statistical method which is usually used as a measure of goodness for the model applied.

In the next section we present LCA model formally.

4.2 A Theoretical Framework

Mathematical models of LCA are well presented in the literature. Here we follow the definitions in [4].

A collection of categorical manifest variables will be distinguished by subscripts and written as a vector

$$x = (x_1,\ x_2,\ \ldots,x_k)$$

where

$$x_i = \begin{cases} 1 \text{ for the positive outcome of the trial} \\ 2 \text{ for the negative outcome of the trial} \end{cases}$$

for $i = 1, 2, \ldots, k$. The outcome corresponding to the code "1" (positive) and to the code "2" (negative) is defined arbitrary.

Considering m latent classes and k dichotomous random variables (categories) the following notations should be introduced.

π_s – the unobserved probability of being in the sth latent class, $s = 1, 2, \ldots, m$;

p_i – observed proportion of sample points that respond positively to the ith dichotomy $(i = 1, 2, \ldots, k)$;

p_{ij} – observed proportion of sample points that respond positively to both the ith and jth dichotomies $(i \neq j, p_{ij} = p_{ji})$;

$p_{ij\ldots k}$ – observed proportion of sample points that respond positively to the ith, jth, ..., kth, dichotomies $(i \neq j \neq \ldots \neq k)$ where permutations of indices are excluded;

ν_{is} – the unobserved conditional probability that a sample point in the sth latent class is also in the ith observed category.

Then the latent class model can be presented as a set of equations:

$$1 = \sum_{s=1}^{m} \pi_s \tag{1}$$

$$p_i = \sum_{s=1}^{m} \pi_s \nu_{is} \tag{2}$$

$$p_{ij} = \sum_{s=1}^{m} \pi_s \nu_{is} \nu_{js} \quad (i, j = 1, 2, \cdots, k) \tag{3}$$

$$p_{ij\cdots k} = \sum_{s=1}^{m} \pi_s \nu_{is} \nu_{js} \cdots \nu_{ls} \quad (i, j, \cdots, l = 1, 2, \cdots, k) \tag{4}$$

where $i \neq j \neq \cdots \neq l$ and permuted subscripts do not appear. Equations (1) - (4) express observed probabilities in terms of unknown probabilities, and represent the general system of normal equations for a latent class model.

A necessary condition for identifiability is

$$\frac{2^k}{k+1} \geq m. \tag{5}$$

The input data for the analysis is the observable variables $p_i, p_{ij}, \ldots, p_{ij\ldots k}$.

5   LCA in the Integration Task

The simplest case of LCA application, illustrated in figure 3, corresponds to the task of integration of two corresponding classes from two different data sources. We have $k = 3$ categories (2 initial and 1 integrated data sources) and $m = 2$ latent classes (an object has only two possibilities: to be a member of RWC or not to be). According to equations (1) - (4) and condition (5) this is the minimal case that could be considered in the LCA.

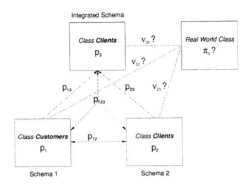

Fig. 3. The integration of two corresponding classes

Let us consider the integration procedure described in the first section and shown in figure 1.

After the first step of integration, namely, defining structure of the input data sources we obtain supports for objects' class membership provided by the applied data mining techniques. For example, we derive a class ***Customers*** in the first data source with support p_1 and a class ***Clients*** with support p_2 in the second data source.

In the next integration step using schema matching and record linkage techniques we find a coefficient of similarity between these two classes p_{12}. Then we integrate these classes to one integrated class ***Clients***.

Basing on the integration result we obtain support value of objects' class membership for this integrated class p_3 as well as similarity coefficient p_{13} between the integrated class ***Clients*** and the class ***Customers*** and a similarity coefficient p_{23} between the integrated class ***Clients*** and the class ***Clients***. Then we get a similarity coefficient for all three classes p_{123}.

Now we would like to know how well both the input and the integrated classes correspond to the real world class (RWC). Let us give some numerical (arbitrary in this example) values to all listed above support and similarity coefficients and see how this task can be solved using LCA. The input data for the LCA is summarized as follows.

$N = 10000$ – the number of objects in each category;
$p_1 = 0.85$ – support of the class ***Customers*** membership;
$p_2 = 0.82$ – support of the class ***Clients*** membership;

$p_3 = 0.87$ – support of the integrated class **Clients** membership;

$p_{12} = 0.72$ – support of membership of the objects in both classes **Customers** and **Clients**;

$p_{13} = 0.78$ – support of membership of the objects in both classes **Customers** and integrated **Clients**;

$p_{23} = 0.77$ – support of membership of the objects in both classes **Clients** and integrated **Clients**;

$p_{123} = 0.70$ – support of membership of the objects in all three classes.

Basing on the input data we construct the matrix of class membership X. It consists of the following combinations:

Pattern	Number of occurrences
$1 - 1 - 1$	7000
$1 - 2 - 1$	800
$2 - 1 - 1$	700
$2 - 2 - 1$	200
$1 - 1 - 2$	200
$1 - 2 - 2$	500
$2 - 1 - 2$	300
$2 - 2 - 2$	300

In the general case the initial data may not fit well to requirements of statistical analysis. For example, a random part of X does not have a zero correlation matrix. That is why we should apply LCA technique that is based on the likelihood-ratio estimation to adopt real data to the statistical model [3]. There are many available LCA realizations (almost in any statistical software package) offering the functionality we need here. In this paper we abstain from going in the theoretical details of these methods. A solution of our integration example (obtained by WinLTA freeware package) is shown below.

$\pi_1 = 0.819$ – the unobserved probability of RWC membership;

$\nu_{11} = 0.919$ – the unobserved conditional probability that the objects from the RWC are also in the class **Customers**;

$\nu_{21} = 0.916$ – the unobserved conditional probability that the objects from the RWC are also in the class **Clients**;

$\nu_{31} = 1.000$ – the unobserved conditional probability that the objects from the RWC are also in the integrated class **Clients**;

$\pi_2 = 0.181$ – the unobserved probability of RWC non-membership;

$\nu_{12} = 0.538$ – the unobserved conditional probability that the objects which are not in RWC are presented in the class **Customers**;

$\nu_{22} = 0.385$ – the unobserved conditional probability that the objects which are not in RWC are presented in the class **Clients**;

$\nu_{32} = 0.281$ – the unobserved conditional probability that the objects which are not in RWC are presented in the integrated class **Clients**.

As a result the LCA gives us an answer to the question how many objects belong to the RWC ($\pi_1 = 0.819$). Indeed, this value demonstrates a confidence with which the objects from all three classes (*Customers*, *Clients* and integrated *Clients*) correspond to RWC.

The classes *Customers* and *Clients* were defined correctly with corresponding probabilities 0.919 and 0.916. The integration of these two classes was performed in a way to include all the RWC objects in the integrated class ($\nu_{31} = 1.000$).

We see that 18.1% of objects do not belong to RWC. The probabilities to find them in the classes *Customers*, *Clients* and integrated class are 0.538, 0.385 and 0.281 correspondingly. This example demonstrates ability of the LCA application with respect to data integration.

Thus we consider the LCA as a powerful statistical method which can be employed to the integration tasks for analyzing the input and output data. It can analyze any relationships between the classes (equivalence, inclusion, intersection, disjointness) and operate with missing data. The LCA provides an evaluation of single integration steps as well as an evaluation of the whole integration process which is mostly important when the initial data contains uncertainties.

6   Conclusion

The crucial question for the integration is the quality of the integrated database. That is how exact the real world entities are presented in it. Our approach presented here is able to answer this question. We have shown how a statistical model of the integration task can be developed. It can be summarized as follows.

The required input data such as support of objects' class membership (p_i), support of class correspondence (p_{ij}) and a result of integration (p_{ijl}) has to be discovered by data mining, schema matching, data cleaning, schema and data integration methods.

Then the output data associated with the unobservable latent factors such as RWC membership is provided by LCA. The method can be applied to each single step of the integration giving us a propagation of uncertainties in the process of integration.

The key parameter is the RWC membership probability (π_1). Its value varies depending on the integration strategy and integration decisions. One can think about maximization of RWC membership probability in order to obtain the highest integration quality. This can be achieved by adjusting the selection criteria used by the methods applied during the integration process.

It is important to emphasize that an integrated database is naturally included in the analysis. Therefore, we can try various strategies of integration and see how they contribute to the probability of RWC membership. Thus, the approach provides a promising technique for optimizing the integration that is subject to future work.

We are also convinced that this technique is a powerful tool for the analysis of decisions taken at every single integration step, especially in difficult, ambiguous cases.

The proposed approach opens a way for an optimal integration of data sources which contain uncertain information.

References

1. E. Altareva and S. Conrad. The Problem of Uncertainty and Database Integration. In R.-D. Kutsche, S. Conrad, and W. Hasselbring, editors, *Proceedings of the 4th Workshop Engineering Federated Information Systems, EFIS 2001, October 9-10, Berlin*, pages 81–92. aka / IOS Press / infix, 2000.
2. E. Altareva and S. Conrad. Dealing with Uncertainties during the Data(base) Integration Process. In Gunnar Weber, editor, *Tagungsband zum 14. GI-Workshop Grundlagen von Datenbanken, Strandhotel Fischland, Halbinsel Fischland-Darß-Zingst, Mecklenburg-Vorpommern, 21. bis 24. Mai 2002*, pages 6–10. Fachbereich Informatik, Universität Rostock, 2002.
3. D. Bartholomew and M. Knott. *Latent Variable Models and Factor Analysis*, volume 7 of *Kendall's Library of Statistics*. Arnold, London, 1999.
4. A. Basilevsky. *Statistical Factor Analysis and Related Methods: Theory and Applications*. Wiley and Sons, New York, 1994.
5. D. Beneventano, S. Bergamaschi, F. Guerra, and M. Vincini. The MOMIS Approach to Information Integration. In *ICEIS 2001, Proc. of the 3rd Int. Conf. on Enterprise Information Systems, Setubal, Portugal, July 7-10, 2001*, 2001.
6. W. Fan, H. Lu, S. E. Madnick, and D. W.-L. Cheung. Discovering and Reconciling Value Conflicts for Numerical Data Integration. *Information Systems*, 26(8):635–656, 2001.
7. D. Hand, H. Mannila, and P. Smyth. *Principles of Data Mining*. MIT Press, Massachusetts Institute of Technology, USA, 2001.
8. W. L. Low, M.-L. Lee, and T. W. Ling. A knowledge-based Approach for Duplicate Elimination in Data Cleaning. *Information Systems*, 26(8):585–606, 2001.
9. L. Palopoli, G. Terracina, and D. Ursino. The System DIKE: Towards the Semi-Automatic Synthesis of Cooperative Information Systems and Data Warehouses. In Y. Masunaga, J. Pokorny, J. Stuller, and B. Thalheim, editors, *Proceedings of Chalenges, 2000 ADBIS-DASFAA Symposium on Advances in Databases and Information Systems, Enlarged Fourth East-European Conference on Advances in Databases and Information Systems, Prague, Czech Republic, September 5-8, 2000*, pages 108–117. Matfyz Press, 2000.
10. E. Rahm and P.A. Bernstein. A Survey of Approaches to Automatic Schema Matching. *VLDB Journal*, 10(4):334–350, 2001.
11. I. Schmitt and G. Saake. Merging Inheritance Hierarchies for Database Integration. In *Proc. of the 3rd IFCIS Int. Conf. on Cooperative Information Systems, CoopIS'98, August 20-22, 1998, New York, USA*, Los Alamitos, CA, 1998. IEEE Computer Society Press.
12. I. Schmitt and C. Türker. An Incremental Approach to Schema Integration by Refining Extensional Relationships. In Georges Gardarin, James C. French, Niki Pissinou, Kia Makki, and Luc Bouganim, editors, *Proceedings of the 1998 ACM CIKM International Conference on Information and Knowledge Management, Bethesda, Maryland, USA, November 3-7, 1998*. ACM Press, 1998.

Storing and Querying Semistructured Data using Relational Databases

Dunren Che and Wen-Chi Hou

Department of Computer Science
Southern Illinois University
Carbondale, IL 62901, U.S.A.
{dche, hou}@cs.siu.edu

Abstract. In this paper, we propose a method of mapping semistructured data to relations and querying the data stored in relational databases. Our approach is based on a graph-based clustering mechanism that groups data items according to their structural relationships into clusters and creates relations corresponding to the identified clusters.

1. Introduction

Semistructured data is ubiquitous. Applications of semistructured data management are diverse. The XML data (or XML document) is one important instance of semistructured data. A federation of multiple heterogeneous data sources is another example of semistructured dataset. For example, University A and University B (see Fig. 1) want to share their faculty and allow their students to take courses from the other university. Both universities thus expect to federate their data sources for supporting this cooperation. As a whole, the result of such a federation of data sources is a semistructured dataset at a higher level. We are interested in the fundamental mechanisms needed for supporting the federation of heterogeneous data sources. One basic issue is how to model the connections between the various data items from these different data sources in a uniform, federated environment.

In this paper, we limit our interest to the techniques for storing and querying semistructured data in relational databases. Furthermore, we use an XML dataset as the carrier for this study. We hope the techniques we develop can be easily adapted for dealing with more general cases about semestructured data, including federation of heterogeneous information sources.

Our mapping approach is not based on DTDs/schemas because XML documents may not have a DTD or may not share the same DTD in a document database, in addition, semistructured data generally do not have the notion of DTDs or schemas.

While a lot of work has been done on semistructured data management [1] [3] [6] [9] in the past, the current interest is in using RDBMS as a platform to store and query XML data [4] [5] [7] [8] [10] [11] [12] [13]. The advantage of using RDBMS includes reusing a mature technology and the seamless inter-access between semistructured data and the legacy relational data in a single system.

Regarding mapping XML data to the relational model, numerous approaches have been proposed. The majority of them were set forth based on an accompanying DTD/schemas [1] [12] [11] [13]. Our approach is independent of any DTD/schema and shall be able to uniformly deal with both DTD-less and DTD-valid XML documents and can be easily adapted for other types of semistructured data.

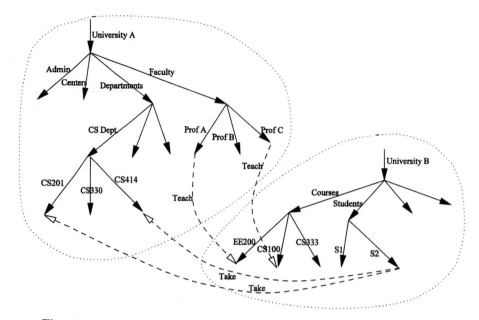

Fig.1. Heterogeneous data source federation represented as semistructured data graph

The remainder of the paper is organized as follows. Section 2 presents our mapping method. Section 3 discusses query translation from XQuery to SQL based on the mapping our approach produces. Section 4 compares our method with related work and Section 5 concludes this discussion and provides an outlook of future work.

2. Mapping XML Documents to Relations

Simply put, a mapping scheme decides which elements of the documents are to be made into separate relations and which elements are to be "inlined" as attributes to existing relations. The decision can only be made reasonably by proper consideration of the structural relationships between document elements. There are plenty of structural properties among elements of structured documents, which can be useful for appropriately grouping elements together and storing them into relations.

Structured documents in general, XML documents in particular, stand for important instances of semistructured data. In the subsequent discussion, we will focus on XML documents regardless of their DTD/schema. A semistructured data set is generally represented as a graph, called a *data graph*. We can derive the so-called *syntax graph* from a data graph by merging multiple occurrences of the same type of nodes in the data graph. Each node in a data graph corresponds to a data item, while each node in a syntax graph represents the type of elements. A type node, as usual, covers one or more concrete elements/items of the source dataset. The elements covered by a type node, say *x*, is referred to as the extent of the type, annotated as *extent(x)*. The syntax graph is a similar concept to the Dataguide of the Lore DBMS system [6]. We will investigate the structural relationships among the nodes in the syntax graph of each XML document to conduct proper mapping of XML data to relational schemas. Fig. 2 is the syntax graph of a synthetic XML document. We choose to use a synthetic one instead of a real world example because it is relatively easier to make up one than find a real one that covers all the features we want to highlight in this discussion.

When a source XML data file is parsed, the structural relationships between element types, as depicted in Fig. 2, are extracted. We are in particular interested in the following five types of nodes, which are mapped to separate relations:

1) The **root** node.

2) **Centrum** nodes, which must have an *out-degree* greater than two. For example, the root node A in Fig. 2 has an out-degree of 6.

3) **Shared** nodes, which must have an *in-degree* greater than 2. For example, the node H in Fig. 2 has an in-degree of 3.

4) **Set-valued** nodes. A node is called *set-valued* if the type's multiple instances are found to consecutively appear within the same enclosing element. For example, multiple elements of the type N in Fig. 2 may consecutively appear in an element of type J, and N is called *set-valued* and annotated as N(s).

5) **Long path leading nodes**. If a node is not identified as any of the above and it leads to a long path (with a length greater than 3), it is called a *long path leading* node (or *path leader* for short). For example, the element type E in Fig. 2 is such a node because it leads to a long path of length 4, E/I/M/O.

We omit the discussion of attributes in this paper because attributes in XML dataset can be treated as a special (simpler) case of elements.

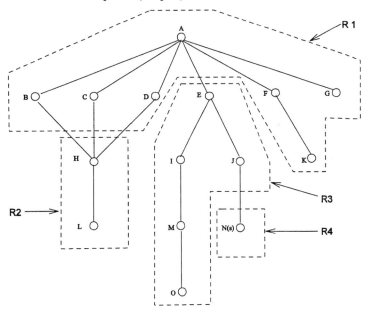

Fig. 2. The syntax graph of a synthetic XML document

Given an XML document of adequate structural complexity, there may exist a huge number (possibly infinite) of configurations of mapping of these elements (and element attributes) to relations (and relation attributes). Let us rationalize the ideas of our mapping approach below. First, the root element in a document is a special element; it is the starting point for navigating the data graph and many queries may be posed just around this node. It is proper to map the root node into a separate relation to facilitate this type of queries. Second, elements with a big out-degree, i.e., Centrum elements, are a natural counterpart of the entity notion of the ER model in the new context of XML data modeling. In our approach, both the attributes and the direct subelements of a Centrum element are inlined into the Centrum element to form a cluster and the cluster is mapped to a relation. Third, if an element type is shared (as a common subelement type of more than two other element types), it is not inlined to either of its parent types, but mapped to a separate relation to avoid duplicated store of the contents of this element type in multiple relations. Fourth, since a relational database does not support set-valued attributes, it is necessary to segregate set-valued element into a separate relation. Fifth, the separation of the long path leader element types from their parent relations is based on the following consideration. Inlining is commonly used to flatten elements into their parent relations for reducing the number of joins needed for executing queries involving long paths. However, over application of this technique easily incurs huge, sparse relations involving highly duplicated store of the same values in many different table rows. The study of Florescu *et al* [5] had revealed the fact that over application of the "inlining" performs very poorly for heavy queries because the huge table thus generated becomes very expensive in this case. Florescu *et al*'s work inspired us to control the application of the inlining technique by adequately exploiting the structural relationships among document elements. While long path leaders are separated from their parents, the paths as a whole are mapped to dedicated relations whenever this is appropriate. In other words, the elements on a long path are collectively stored in a single relation that serves as pre-stored joins for queries involving the path.

Our mapping algorithm generates two types of relations: *o-relation* (ordinary relations) and *t-relation* (temporary relations) and ends up with only o-relations. The temporary t-relations are used during the mapping process to help accomplish our mapping strategy. A special attribute, *plength*, is added to each t-relation to keep track of the length of the longest path so far accommodated by the t-relation. The plength attribute is updated whenever a new branch (a different path) is inlined.

Our algorithm is described at a high level as below:

1. While an XML document is parsed, the information about the elements and the relationships among the elements are extracted and recorded in an *element type table*, called *ETT* with the following columns: *element-name, parent-name, is-root, in-degree, out-degree, set-valued, depth*, and *visited*.

2. Sort the *ETT* table in non-increasing order of the depth column values.

3. Scan the *ETT* table, if an *unvisited* entry is the *root*, or has an *in-degree* greater than 2, or *out-degree* greater than 2, or is *set-valued*, create an o-relation for the corresponding element type and mark the entry as *visited*.

4. Scan the *ETT* table for 2nd pass and do the following for each unvisited entry:

   1) if the entry's parent is *visited*, skip;

   2) otherwise, create a t-relation for its parent and inline it into the t-relation just created, and mark both the child and parent entry as *visited*;

   3) trace back to the parent's parent, if the grandparent is *unvisited*, create a t-relation for it and inline the parent's t-relation into this new t-relation;

   4) repeat step 2) and 3) until we meet a parent that is *visited* and an o-relation has been created for it (during this process, the number of inlines performed are recorded in the *plength* attribute of each t-relation).

5. Scan *ETT* table for the 3rd time, inline any *unvisited* entry into its parent.

6. (Now all entries are *visited* and two types of relations are created: o-relations and t-relations) review each t-relation by doing the following:

    1) if its *plength* is less than 3, inline the t-relation into its parent relation;

    2) otherwise, convert the t-relation as an o-relation.

During the above process, our algorithm scans the *ETT* table three times. The first time, it creates relations for the *root* element type, *Centrum* element types, *shared* element types, and *set-valued* element types. The second time, it identifies *long path leading nodes* and creates relations to accommodate these paths. The third time, it inlines all unvisited element types into their parent or ancestors. In the meanwhile, the algorithm keeps a record of the mappings performed that form an *element type dictionary* (*ETD* for short) per document. The *ETD* is needed to translate XQuery into SQL format and reconstruct SQL query result according to XML format.

In addition to the attribute generated for each inlined subelement in an o-relation, our mapping algorithm automatically generates two extra attributes in the relation: *Id* and *Pid* (parent id). Pid serves as a foreign key into its parent relation. Furthermore, a third extra attribute, called "*Petn*", i.e., the parent's element type name, may be added to a relation, if the parent is inlined into a further higher level. The Petn attribute simply holds the element type name (*etn* for short) of its parent so that our query engine later can rebuild exactly the connection between the elements in this relation and their parent elements in another relation. No foreign key is generated for the root relation.

To illustrate our method, we work with the following example of a synthetic XML document complying with the syntax graph given in Fig. 2.

Example source XML data

```
<A>
  <B>
    <H>
      <L>
         Content of L1
      </L>
    </H>
  </B>
  <C>
    <H>
      <L>
         Content of L2
      </L>
    </H>
  </C>
  <D>
    <H>
      <L>
         Content of L3
      </L>
    </H>
  </D>
  <E>
    <I>
      <M>
        <O>
```

```
            Content of O
           </O>
          </M>
        </I>
        <J>
          <N>
            Content of N1
          </N>
          <N>
            Content of N2
          </N>
          <N>
            Content of N3
          </N>
        </J>
      </E>
      <F>
        <K>
          Content of K
        </K>
      </F>
      <G>
        Content of G
      </G>
    </A>
```

Our algorithm generates the following relations:

R 1

Id	A	B	C	D	F	K	G
R1_1							

R 3

Id	Pid	E	I	M	O	J
R3_1	R1_1					

R 2

Id	Pid	Petn	H	L
R2_1	R1_1	B		Content of L1
R2_2	R1_1	C		Content of L2
R2_3	R1_1	D		Content of L3

R 4

Id	Pid	Petn	N
R4_1	R3_1	J	Content of N1
R4_2	R3_1	J	Content of N1
R4_3	R3_1	J	Content of N1

Note that when dealing with XML data using our approach, *recursion* is no longer an issue of concern because our algorithm does not rely on DTD and the cycle incurred by recursion at the type level is naturally broken. Furthermore, if an element type has neither atomic value nor attributes but merely servers as a container of other (sub-) elements, the relation corresponding to this element type does not actually need to have a designated attribute for this element type. For example, if element types B, C, and D do not have atomic values but just serve as containers of H elements, then they do not need explicitly to appear as designated attributes in relation R1. However, for uniformity and ease of discussion, we keep a position for all elements in their relations regardless of whether they have atomic values or not.

Documents in our database

do not have to comply with a common DTD/schema. However, familiar element types like name, address, paragraph, footnote, etc. may be broadly shared among many different documents. If they take the same structure, they will eventually share the same relations in our system. Furthermore, due to irregular use of tag names in different documents, name conflict is inevitable, which is resolved in our approach by choosing a different name for a relation or relation attribute if conflict indeed arises.

That is why in our element type dictionary we need to keep a record of the target (a relation or a relation attribute) that each element type is mapped to (see the element type dictionary example in Section 3).

With our approach, we intentionally take the principles of the ER model into account and create relations for entities (i.e., clusters of strongly structure-related elements in our case).

It is helpful to point out that XML data, although is regarded as a type of semistructured data, does not posses all the characters of general semistructured data. First, the XML data graph is a neat (nested) hierarchy while the data graph of semistructured data is a graph. Second, a semistructured dataset may not be specified using the same format as an XML document. Therefore, there still is nontrivial work for adapting our approach to the cases of more general semistructured data. For example, we need a new mechanism to build the ETT (element type table) from a data source that is not specified according to the XML standard. Additionally, we have to deal with possible circles in the data graph of general semistructured data.

3. XML Query Processing

The query language we choose to support in our system is XQuery [2], the latest proposal for a standard XML query language. In our setting, XQuery queries are first optimized and then translated into SQL format for evaluation. XML query optimization is a major topic in our research. It is best performed before queries are translated to SQL because the rich semantics of XML queries is only available at the XQuery level. Our optimization investigation focuses on exploiting the structural knowledge of the XML documents and enabling the application of potential structure indexes that may be superficially inapplicable.

During query translation, we need to access the knowledge of how XML data is mapped to relations and attributes, which is available from the *ETD* (*element type dictionary*). The ETD contains one entry for each element type (corresponding to a distinct tag name). Each ETD entry contains the *id* of the document (doc-id), a tag name, a relation name, and an attribute name (If an element type does not appear in the relation as an attribute, i.e., it is directly mapped to the relation, then the attribute name column takes the NULL value).

As an example, we give the ETD corresponding to the above mapping example (next page).

The XQuery language is designed to be broadly applicable across many types of XML data sources. An XQuery query (*X query* for short) is typically posed against a single context document introduced by the *document( )* function [2]. We introduce a default context for queries in a document database environment, which is indicated by the keyword "any" and refers to the entire set of documents in the database.

ETD Table

doc-id	tag name	relation name	attribute name
1	A	R1	A
1	B	R1	B
1	C	R1	C
1	D	R1	D
1	E	R3	E
1	F	R1	F
1	G	R1	G
1	H	R2	H
1	I	R3	I
1	J	R3	J
1	K	R1	K
1	L	R2	L
1	M	R3	M
1	N	R4	N

We use the two query examples below to illustrate how XQuery translation in our system.

1. Find all H elements that can be reached by path /A/C/H.

2. Find all N elements that are contained in a J element.

According to XQuery syntax, these queries are formulated as follows.

X Query 1.

```
FOR $h IN Any/A/C/H
RETURN
<H>
      $h
</H>
```

X Query 2.

```
FOR $n IN Any//J/N
RETURN
<N>
      $h
</N>
```

Due to space limitation, we provide a simplified version of our algorithm that transforms X queries to SQL format. The major steps of this algorithm are the following.

1. Identify all document paths involved in an X query, including single node paths; the result is a path set (paths involved in an X query are called *Xpaths*).

2. Simplify the Xpath set by removing duplications. For example, suppose we have an Xpath set, *{author, book.author.name, person.child.person.name}*, the single node path *author* in the set can be removed because it is already covered by the second path in the set but none of the two occurrences of the *person* tag in the third path should be removed (which is a recursive one).

3. Convert Xpaths as *Jpaths* (*join paths*) by introducing relevant table names (The Xpath translation is not trivial, considering that table aliases may be introduced for dealing with name conflicts during mapping).

4. The *where* clause of XQuery directly translates to the *where* clause of SQL with tag names being substituted by corresponding table/attribute names.

5. The *Jpath set* translates to a SQL *from* clause (The keyword JOIN may be introduced.)

6. The *return* clause of XQuery translates to a *select* clause. Subelement interpolation is enforced only if the subelement is inlined.

Our translated SQL queries return only *flat* results at the time. X queries generally produce results in a tree-like structure. To meet this requirement, the results of SQL queries need to be repacked before being delivered to end-users. Due to space limitation, we omit further discussion of this issue.

According to the above transformation algorithm, the two X query examples are translated to the following SQL queries:

SQL Query 1.

```
SELECT  R2.H
FROM    R1 JOIN R2 ON R1.Id = R2.Pid
WHERE   R2.Pen = "C"
```

SQL Query 2.

```
SELECT  R4.N
FROM    R3 JOIN R4 ON R3.Id = R4.Pid
WHERE   R4.Pen = "J"
```

This simplified version of X query transformation algorithm successfully rewrites most of the X queries we tested into correct SQL format.

4. Comparison with Related Work

Although a lot of work on mapping XML documents to a relational schema has been published, only a few are closely related to our method – mapping without relying on DTDs. In this section, we make a comparison with some notable methods.

Alin Deutsch et al [1] informally defined a "good" mapping as one that minimizes disk space, reduces data fragmentation and satisfies constraints of the RDBMS (e.g., maximum number of attributes per relation). The first two of these criteria are actually contradictory with each other. "Minimizing disk space" asks for a highly normalized schema, and both the *edge table approach* and the *attribute approach* in [5] are at this extreme, which, however maximizes data fragmentation. The *universal table approach* in [5] is at the other extreme, which minimizes data fragmentation but may maximize data redundancy and introduce highly sparse tables. Regarding query processing, the two criteria are also contradictory, e.g., the *edge table approach* [5] has to pay a high cost for many joins needed for evaluating a query, while the *universal table approach* [5] generally gets a good performance because all joins are "pre-stored". So in essence, a "good" mapping is to find a good tradeoff between "minimizing disk space" and "minimizing data fragmentation" under the constraints of the RDBMS used. Floroscu et al [12] addressed the two extremes, but did not show how to find a good tradeoff. They also indicated that the "value inline" idea is always a good one, which is also adopted by our approach.

Shanmugasundaram et al [12] introduced an approach that starts from simplifying a given DTD, generates a relational schema based on the DTD, parses the XML documents conforming to the DTD and then shreds them into tuples fitting the relational schema. The "basic" idea in [12] is to inline as many descendant elements as possible into the table created for one element type. This idea technically resembles the *universal table* idea. To reduce the high redundancy problem, the authors later on introduced two variants of the "basic" approach: "shared" and "hybrid". Shanmugasundaram et al [12] did not address how to approach a possible "good" tradeoff. Furthermore, their methods only work with XML documents with DTDs.

Of the many mapping approaches proposed, we think the work in [5] and the work in [12] are quite representative. Both use mainly the same technique, inlining, but the former deals with all documents regardless of DTD, while the latter only cope with documents with a DTD. Let us use the two contradictory criteria of a "good" mapping, i.e., minimizing data redundancy and minimizing data fragmentation as a frame and put the various approaches proposed in [5] and [12] into this frame. We get a figurative illustration of the various approaches in Fig. 3. In our approach, we have made an effort to exploit structural relationships among document elements to cluster elements together and map them to relations. We expect our approach will bring us much closer to a "good" mapping.

The method in [11] seems to be a directly improved version of the techniques in [5]. It approaches the same problem from the syntax graph representation of an XML document. The data model it follows is based on a complete binary fragmentation of the document tree. According to this method, all the associations of the same type (under the same path) are stored in the same binary relation. Each relation takes the path as its name. It indeed clustered the element-subelement relations according to their common paths. However, the number of tables (implying joins) is too big. In addition, as the document structure is decomposed into binary relations, XML queries usually translate into SQL statements with an excessive number of joins.

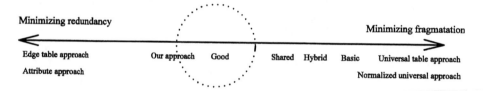

Fig. 3. Tradeoff between minimizing data fragmentation and minimizing data redundancy

The approach adopted by the Lego project [13] represents one of the most recent advances in achieving XML-to-relation mapping. The LegoDB mapping engine generates alternative configurations (mapping schemes) through XML-schema rewritings and selects the best one based on estimated cost with regard to a given application. Again, the LegoDB approach depends on schemas and does not work with schema-less documents. Furthermore, the LegoDB approach produces a "best" scheme based on a given type of application. For different applications, the chosen scheme may be a bad one. It is doubtful whether it is practical to keep multiple mapping schemes for one set of data and duplicate the data in multiple databases or when application changes to redo the mapping and regenerate the whole database.

5. Conclusions and Future Work

In this paper, we presented a new method of mapping semistructured data, specifically the XML data, to the relational schema. Our method does not rely on any existing DTD or XML schema – this well fits the *schema-less* characteristic of semistructured data. With semistructured data management, paths are of special interest. Our method identifies in particular a class of nodes that are the leader nodes of long paths. All the nodes on a long path are mapped to the same relation. So, joins between these nodes are avoided during query evaluation. As our approach takes into account the structural relationships among data items for clustering, it does not suffer between these nodes are avoided during query evaluation. As our approach takes into account the structural relationships among data items for clustering, it does not suffer from either of the two drawbacks indicated above, i.e., over-fragmentation and over-inlining, which, however, are common to many previous approaches[5][11][12]. The number of relations generated by our approach is moderate.

Primarily, the XML data assumes the form of 1:n hierarchies that our algorithm effectively clusters. For dealing with more general semistructured data (involving m:n cases), we can easily adapt our algorithm to identify the m:n cases during XML data parsing and generate separate relations corresponding to the m:n relationships, or attain the same goal by adding a suffix step of normalization. It should be self-evident that the output relations of our algorithms are in 3NF.

Currently, our project is continuing, and only limited tests have been done, but the result is encouraging. As future work, we plan to make the thresholds used for deciding long paths, Centrum nodes, and shared nodes adjustable. We may also identify more structural patterns among the data items of a semistructured data set. These patterns could indicate further improved mapping with regard to storage and query efficiencies. XQuery optimization is yet another major interest of us.

References

1. A. Deutsch, M. Fernandez, and D. Suciu. "Storing Semistructured Data with STORED". In Proc. of ACM SIGMOD, pp. 431-442, 1999.
2. S. Boag, D. Chamberlin, M. F. Fernandez, Daniela Florescu, J. Robie, J. Siméon, M. Stefanescu, "XQuery 1.0: An XML Query Language", WX Working Draft, www.w3.org /fR/xquery/.
3. M. Fernandez and D. Suciu. "Optimizing Regular Path Expressions Using Graph schemas". In Proc. of IEEE International Conference on Data Engineering, 1998.
4. M. Fernandez, W. Tan, D. Suciu. "SilkRoute: Trading between Relations and XML". In Proc. of 9th Int. World Wide Web Conf. (WWW), Amsterdam, May, 2000
5. D. Florescu, and D. Kossmann. "Storing and Querying XML Data Using an RDMBS". IEEE Data Engineering Bulletin 22(3), pp. 27-34, 1999.
6. R. Goldman and J. Widom. "DataGuides: enabling query formulation and optimization in semistructured databases". In Proc. of the Conference on Very Large Data Bases, 1997.
7. G. Kappel, E. Kapsammer, W. Retschitzegger. "X-Ray -Towards Integrating XML and Relational Database Systems". In Proc. of Int'l conf. On Conceptual Modeling (ER). Salt Lake City, UT. October 2000
8. M. Klettke, H. Meyer. "XML and Object-Relational Database Systems - Enhancing Structural Mappings Based on Statistics". Int. Workshop on the Web and Databases (WebDB), Dallas, May, 2000
9. J. McHugh, S. Abiteboul, R. Goldman, D. Quass, and J. Widom. "Lore: A Database Management System For Semistructured Data". SIGMOD Record, 1997.
10. I. Tatarinov, S. Viglas, K. Beyer, J. etc. "Storing and Querying Ordered XML Using a Relational Database System". In ACM SIGMOD. 2002
11. A. Schmidt, M. Kersten, M. Windhouwer, and F. Waas. "Efficient Relational Storage and Retrieval of XML Documents". In Proc. of WebDB. pp. 47-52, 2000.
12. J. Shanmugasundaram, K. Tufte, G. He, C. Zhang, D. DeWitt, and J. Naughton. "Relational Databases for Querying XML Documents: Limitations and Opportunities". In Proc. of VLSB, pp. 302-314, 1999.
13. P. Bohannon, J. Freire, P. Roy, J. Siméon. "From XML schema To Relations: A Cost-Based Approach to XML Storage". In Proc. of the 18th International Conference on Data Engineering (ICDE'02).

Semantic Replication in Mobile Federated Information Systems*

Hagen Höpfner and Kai-Uwe Sattler

Otto-von-Guericke-University of Magdeburg
Department of Computer Science
P.O. Box 4120, 39016 Magdeburg, Germany
{hoepfner|sattler}@iti.cs.uni-magdeburg.de

Abstract. Mobile information systems integrating information from different sources and feed mobile clients represent a big challenge for todays DBMS technology. Due to the limited capabilities of the clients (available memory, usable bandwidth, temporary disconnections etc.) traditional replication approaches known from distributed databases fail. In this paper we present an approach for data replication that considers the mobility of clients: The data sets which have to be replicated to mobile clients depend often on dynamic parameters like location of the client or time. Therefore, we introduce a generic model for specifying fragments of the global database with respect to such parameters.

1 Introduction

The increasing availability of mobile devices and wireless communication technologies opens new applications which can improve services by providing real-time access to remote information sources. Examples of such applications are not only stock tickers or messenger applications but also mobile hospital information systems and car navigation systems. However, due to the mobile and wireless nature of these devices, several limitations have to be taken into account in developing and running such mobile information systems: (1) The structure of the network as well as the availability of mobile nodes are subject to continuous changes. (2) The bandwidth of the communication channels is – compared to traditional wired networks – relatively low and communication is much more expensive. (3) The resources of mobile devices, e.g. memory and computing power, are strictly limited.

For a mobile information system, the first two properties prohibit data access by only remote querying. Thus, the mobile device should keep a copy of the data that is the subject of the current operations. The third issue restricts the data managed locally on the mobile device to a subset of the overall (remote) database. This raises the need for *semantic replication*: data that is relevant in a certain situation has to be transfered to the mobile device and in case of local updates the modifications are propagated back to the main database.

A main issue in this context is the reduction of the replicated data in order to meet the requirements of minimal resource consumption (storage space, transfer time or volume). One approach for reducing the amount of data transfered to the mobile device is

---

* This research is supported by the DFG under grant SA 782/3-2

based on dynamic parameters (*replication criteria*) like the current time or location of the device. Here, these parameters are used to pre-select the relevant data at the server-side before replicating it. A possible application is an advanced car driver information system. In addition to street maps stored on a local disk the mobile system retrieves further information about local (i.e., relevant to the current location and time) traffic spots, accidents, detours etc. from a federated database integrating these informations from various sources and displays it to the user or uses it for other operations, e.g. route planning. When this information becomes irrelevant, it can be removed from the local database. This scenario could be extended to support updates – a driver reports an accident or the system detects a traffic jam automatically – as well as other kinds of parameters, for example the kind of car (truck, automobile).

In this paper we present a replication approach which is based on semantic extensions of the global view. Using this approach, location-based services and services requiring replication depending on dynamic features can be easily (on the global view level) implemented. It is embedded into the context of mobility. While looking at related work we can not consider all requirements caused by the special characteristics of mobile computing. Therefore, we focus on work related to replication in mobile information systems.

Some simple problems like position dependent replication (as shown in [LLS00]) are resolvable with views or snapshots known from commercial lightweight database management systems such as Oracle 9*i* lite or IBM's DB2 everyplace. But mobile nodes must explicitly know the necessary location information format used on the database server.

The adaptive replication scheme published in [WC99] uses history information to predefine user specific replicas. Explicit hints about users mobility and access patterns are collected as schedules. Here, the location information are extracted from the cell in which the mobile host is included. Their history is used to pre-calculate possible relevant data.

Beside these researches, our work overlaps with semantic caching. In [RD99] a semantic caching mechanism is presented. The results of queries are cached in form of clustered semantic segments which are comparable to our fragmentation functions[1]. But they are restricted to the projection and the selection of tuples of a single relations. Our approach provides a more flexible definition of fragments resp. segments and is not limited to location awareness.

2 Foundations

The basic network model is based on [PS98]. Mobile hosts have a wireless connection to a base station. This base station is connected to a wired network of fixed hosts. The idea is, that the mobile host sends information about its context (e.g. "I am in London.") to the base station where they are used for selecting fragments, which are relevant for the mobile host.

Therefore, parts of the database on the base stations are enhanced by additional information (e.g. position, time). These extended parts are called *fragments*, and the

---

[1] They constitute semantic parts (fragments) of a database.

additional information are called *extensions*. In fact, fragments can contain almost arbitrary segments of one or more qrelation(s) and my be overlapping.

Because we try to reduce the necessary additional information, extensions v_{name}, which are vectors[2] representing the used context elements (e.g. two dimensional geographic coordinates $v_{gc}(x, y)$ $x, y \in \mathbb{R}$), are divided into *server extensions* $v_{name}^{se} \in \mathcal{V}_{se}$ and *client extensions* $v_{name}^{ce} \in \mathcal{V}_{ce}$. So, the fragments on the base node are extended by a set of server extensions. For choosing the relevant fragments for replication the client extensions are compared to the stored server extensions. The difference between server and client extensions is the complexity of the parameters (in the example above x and y). While on the server site the parameters may be functions which compute the parameter value, the parameters of client extensions must be constant values. Therefore, server extensions allow to reuse data already stored in databases which are integrated into the global view in addition to the actual data. Moreover, the parameter functions can be used for converting parameters (e.g., converting the GPS-coordinates into the name of the corresponding town).

Because of the given space limitations we assume that server extensions are defined manually. But, we could also learn them from given database queries. Here, generalised queries describe the fragments and the context information transmitted in addition to the queries are used as server extensions. Another approach is the reuse of information of the integrated data sources. Especially in case of sensor databases, the location of the sensors can be used for annotating fragments.

Client extensions are submitted in the form of replication criteria to the base node without any knowledge about the data in the database. This is necessary because not only exact results but also results with a defined variance must be supported. Therefore, a replication criterion consists of a client extension and the minimal postulated and the maximal allowed threshold value. The use of a maximal allowed threshold is intuitive. The minimal postulated threshold allows the replication of additional information. This is especially useful for applications with geographical information. For example, if a mobile node already contains information of its location and wants to expand its horizon, it is obviously less expensive to replicate only the new data.

While specifying the relevant fragments extension-dependent ξ-functions are used. They compute the "distance" between the client extension and the server extension. If this value is greater than or equal to the minimal postulated threshold and lower than or equal to the maximal allowed threshold the respective fragment will be replicated. However, a ξ-function must not necessarily have the properties of a distance function, e.g., has not to be symmetric in the arguments.

Basing on the relational model of Codd [Cod70] and the assumption that REL is the set of all relations in the database our approach can be formally defined as follows: (1) A *parameter function* ψ is defined as mapping $\psi : REL \rightarrow \bigcup_{A \in R} dom(A)$. Ψ is the set of all parameter-functions. In fact, a parameter function is a query which returns a single value. (2) A *server extension* is defined as a vector $v_{name}^{se} = (\psi_0, \cdots, \psi_i)$ with the type identifier (*name*) and ψ_i ($i \in \mathbb{N}$) parameter functions which are used to calculate the values of the extension parameters. $\mathcal{V}_{se}$ is the set of all server extensions. (3) A *client extension* v_{name}^{ce} is a server extension with the additional restriction that the

---

[2] identified by *name*

38

parameter functions ψ_i are constant values. $\mathcal{V}_{ce}$ is the set of all client extensions. (4) A *fragmentation function* $f : REL \rightarrow REL$ is defined as a mapping $f(r(R)) = r'(R')$ with $R' \subseteq R$ and $r'(R') \subseteq \pi_{R'}(r(R))$. (5) A *fragment* of a relational database is defined as $\mathcal{F} = (f, V)$ with the fragmentation function f and a set of server extensions $V = \{v_0, \cdots, v_n\}$ with $n \in \mathbb{N}$ and $v_0, \cdots, v_n \in \mathcal{V}_{se}$. (6) A ξ-*function* $\xi_a(v_{a_1}, v_{a_2})$ is a mapping $\mathcal{V}_{se} \times \mathcal{V}_{ce} \rightarrow \mathbb{R}$ from a server extension $v_{a_1} \in \mathcal{V}_{se}$ and a client extension $v_{a_2} \in \mathcal{V}_{ce}$ to a float value d which describes the "distance" between v_{a_1} and v_{a_2}. Ξ is the set of all ξ-functions. (7) A *replication criterion* is defined as the triple $rk = (v', \Delta^{min}, \Delta^{max})$ with the client extension $v' \in \mathcal{V}_{ce}$ and the threshold values Δ^{max}, $\Delta^{min} \in \mathbb{R}$ ($\Delta^{max} \geq \Delta^{min}$) of the allowed variance of this client extension.

2.1 Examples for extensions and ξ-functions

The approach presented in this paper is a general and flexible way to restrict data which has to be replicated. In this section some examples for extensions and the respective ξ-functions are shown. Because of the given space limitations we consider only the use of time and positioning informations. But other extensions like group memberships (e.g. for queries like: "Give me all information about free rooms in the building i am currently in.") are compatible with our approach, too.

Methods for ascertaining the position of mobile nodes like GPS [Kap96] are widely-used and were detailed investigated considering their usability for various aspects of mobile information systems (e.g. [IN99]). Assuming that the respective extension is given as[3] $v_{gc} = (x, y)$ and the thresholds are $\Delta_{gc}^{min} = b$, $\Delta_{gc}^{max} = c$ of figure 1 illustrates the resulting cases.

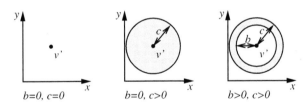

$b=0, c=0$ $b=0, c>0$ $b>0, c>0$

Fig. 1. Peculiarities of the geographic coordinates extension

Obviously, here the ξ-function for two geographic coordinate extensions $v_{gc_1}(x_1, y_1)$ and $v_{gc_2}(x_2, y_2)$ is the Euclidean distance $\sqrt{(x_1 - x_2)^2 + (y_1 - y_2)^2}$. Case c is especially useful, if the mobile host already holds information about its current position and wants to expand the region it is interested in.

A parameter which is often used for restricting range of data is time. Here, the factor time is represented as the interval $[\Delta_{Time}^{max}, \Delta_{Time}^{min}]$. The ξ-function for two time extension $v_{Time_1} = (a)$ and $v_{Time_2} = (b)$ is $\xi_{Time}(v_{Time_1}, v_{Time_2}) = a - b$. Therewith we have three cases:

---

[3] In this example the height (above sea level) is ignored for simplification.

1. $v_{Time} = (a)$, $\Delta_{Time}^{min} = b$, $\Delta_{Time}^{max} = c$ (a, b, c are time values)
   Here, only data with respect to the time interval $[a+b, a+c]$ are taken into account.
   Table 1 contains the resulting special cases.
2. $v_{Time} = (a)$ $\Delta_{Time}^{min} = b = -\infty$, $\Delta_{Time}^{max} = c$
   Only data with respect to the point of time $a+c$ are taken into account. (cf. Table 1)
3. $v_{Time} = (a)$ $\Delta_{Time}^{max} = c = \infty$, $\Delta_{Time}^{min} = b$
   Only data with respect to a point of time from $a + b$ are taken into account. (cf. Table 1)

b	c	Meaning
0	0	Frag. with respect to point of time a
0	> 0	Frag. with respect to point of time between a and c
< 0	0	Frag. with respect to point of time between b and a in the past
< 0	> 0	Frag. with respect to point of time between b and c
> 0	> 0	Frag. with respect to coming point of time between $a + b$ and $a + c$
< 0	< 0	Frag. with respect to point of time between $a - |b|$ and $a - |c|$ in the past
$\neq 0$	$= b$	Frag. with respect to point of time b (a not necessary)
$-\infty$	0	Frag. with respect to point of time until a (incl. a)
$-\infty$	> 0	Frag. with respect to point of time until c (incl. c, a)
$-\infty$	< 0	Frag. with respect to point of time c (incl. c but excl. a because $c < (a+c)$)
0	∞	Frag. with respect to point of time from a
< 0	∞	Frag. with respect to point of time from b (incl. a)
> 0	∞	Frag. with respect to point of time from b (excl. a because $(b + a) > a$)
$-\infty$	∞	Everything (ignore time extension)

Table 1. Usability of the time extension

2.2 Preselection Algorithm

The Algorithm for computing the optimal replica for a mobile host (see algorithm 1) is performed on the base host. Its inputs are a set of replication criteria and the corresponding fragments which are defined in the database. A replication criterion $rk = (v_a^{ce}, \Delta_a^{max}, \Delta_a^{min})$ corresponds with a fragment $\mathcal{F} = (f, V)$ if $\exists v_a^{se} \in V$. That means that the fragment was enhanced by a server extension of the type a. The algorithm returns the set of fragments which are relevant for the mobile host.

Algorithm 1: *Preselection Algorithm*

ENSURE: *INPUT: fragments, set of replication criteria*
ENSURE: *RETURN=$\emptyset$; // reset return set*

01. **for each** $rk_i = (v', \Delta^{max}, \Delta^{min})$ **do**
02.   **for each** fragment $\mathcal{F}_j = (f, V)$ **do**
03.   **if** $\exists(v_n \in V | v_n$ is compatible to $v')$ **then**

04.   **if** $\Delta^{min} \leq \xi_v(v_n, v') \leq \Delta^{max}$ **then** $RETURN = \mathcal{F}_j \cup RETURN$

05. **done**; **done**

06. **return**($RETURN$);

Surely, this algorithm is performed query driven like in other approaches, too. Here that means, that a mobile host sends a request in form of replication criteria to the base station where then the respective set of fragments is computed. But the queries may be easily generated automatically, e.g. location dependent when the mobile host is moving. So, an automatic actualisation of the data on online mobile hosts is supported by our approach as well as replication for often disconnected hosts. Because of the given space limitation we can not work out this characteristics of our semantic replication approach here in more detail.

3 Summary and Conclusions

In this paper we have presented an approach for the reduction of data which has to be transferred between mobile client and database server. The advantage of the presented replication method is the ability of the server to calculate automatically the best replica for the mobile node which has subscribed for data from this server. No user interaction is required to define which data has to be exchanged. Due to the reduction of the volume of data time and cost reduction for transmissions over slow, leased, wireless lines can be achieved. To realize this functionality the global view on the base station which integrates different data sources is divided into fragments, which are marked with information about their relevance for mobile hosts with different attributes. We call these attributes and the fragment marks extensions.

We have explained the foundations of our approach, formally defined the used terms and gave two examples for the usage of extensions and ξ-functions.

References

[Cod70] E. F. Codd. A relational model of data for large shared data banks. *CACM*, 13(6):377–387, 1970.

[IN99] T. Imielinski and J. C. Navas. GPS-based geographic addressing, routing, and resource discovery. *Communications of the ACM*, 42(4):86–92, April 1999.

[Kap96] E. D. Kaplan. *Understanding GPS : Principles and Applications*. Artech House Telecommunications Library. Artech House, March 1996.

[LLS00] K. C. K. Lee, H. V. Leong, and A. Si. Incremental View Maintance for Mobile Databases. *Knowledge and Information Systems*, 2:413–437, 2000.

[PS98] E. Pitoura and G. Samaras. *Data Management for Mobile Computing*. Kluwer Academic Publishers, Boston/Dordrecht/London, 1998.

[RD99] Q. Ren and M. H. Dunham. Using clustering for effective management of a semantic cache in mobile computing. In *Proc. of ACM MobiDE*, pages 94–101. ACM Press, 1999.

[WC99] S. Wu and Y. Chang. An active replication scheme for mobile data management. In A. L. P. Chen and F. H. Lochovsky, editors, *Proc. of the 6th DASFAA*, pages 143–150. IEEE Computer Society, 1999.

A Collaborative Platform for Interoperability of CSCW Applications

Rahat Iqbal, Anne James, Richard Gatward

School of Mathematics and Information Sciences, Coventry University,
CV1 5FB, England

{r.iqbal, a.james, r.a.richard}@coventry.ac.uk

Abstract. Many organisations rely on a wide variety of collaborative applications in order to support their every day activities and to share resources. The collaborative applications are typically designed from scratch if the existing applications do not meet organisational needs. This incurs significant costs, and inconvenience. This paper reports on work concerning the integration of existing collaborative applications or computer supported cooperative work (CSCW) in order to support collaborative activities of organisations. This is a part of our research towards investigating and developing an integrative framework for CSCW applications. It will be flexible enough to accommodate the various and varying needs of the organisation's community. We discuss different types of integration model and interoperability in CSCW and consider different models of CSCW systems. A framework for CSCW integration is presented. An example application scenario involving integration of asynchronous application of our university is discussed.

1 Introduction and Motivation

Collaborative applications are typically designed from scratch if existing applications do not meet organisational needs. At present, CSCW systems tend to be independent and closed [3], [8]. When a new system or application is acquired or developed it is not possible to use it with existing systems. This is a major limitation.

Currently, CSCW applications ignore the existence of other applications [3], [8], [17] and the benefits that could otherwise be brought to an enterprise. The detail of the problem is described in [8]. Thus, there is a demand for the integration of existing CSCW and/or legacy applications. The main benefit of an integrative framework is the support of interoperability between heterogeneous systems.

An open CSCW system is required, which supports a wide range of applications and a variety of cooperative users [17]. To make all the applications work together a platform is required that can maintain a collection of heterogeneous applications, paradigms and models [3], [17]. This should provide interoperability among different applications running locally or remotely at different platforms supporting synchronous or asynchronous activity. This should allow the users of these applications to register an activity or a group of activities to share with other users and applications. Such a CSCW system can meet the requirements of all the users [3]. It is likely that great improvement in productivity will be gained if applications can be integrated. This has motivated our work towards the development of a framework for the integration of CSCW applications.

This paper describes work carried out at Coventry University towards the development of an integrative framework for CSCW. Section 2 describes different levels of integration and interoperability. Section 3 presents our framework of integration. Section 4 describes an integrative model. Section 5 presents applications scenarios to demonstrate the framework for integration. Section 6 discusses the work and provides some conclusions. This section also outlines some points for future research.

2 Levels of Integration

Different levels of integration are possible. At one level two autonomous systems may interoperate by passing data to each other either directly or through a common "blackboard" area. Thus activities in one application may be affected by information received from other applications but integration here is at a loose level of coupling and may be termed surface integration. A deeper level of integration would involve merging or consolidating some activities or resources. This process may involve resolving conflicts between comparable activities or resources in different systems. A complete integration would involve the making one single system from underlying systems where all conflicts among activities or application objects have been resolved. Table 1 summarises the three levels of integration. At levels two and three, the question of virtual or real integration arises. At these levels both real or virtual integration is possible. In the case of the latter mappings would need to exist from a conceptual integrated model to underlying physical applications.

Table 1: Levels of Integration

Level	Type	Description
3 (Complete Integration)	Fully Integrated	All system models resolved and fully integrated.
2 (Deep Integration)	Tightly Coupled	Some aspects of the system models are integrated but not all
1 (Surface Integration)	Loosely Coupled	Independent systems communicate through messages or shared areas or service middleware

It is worth noting that surface integration can be achieved easily using current technology at the level of service provision. A CSCW system that wishes to make its functionality and information available publicly can do so by participating in distributed system services such as CORBA or Web Services. However such systems provide integration or interoperability only at a syntactic level. Semantic detail concerning real-world understanding of what the CSCW system does and what information it has, is not supported. Thus the use of this type of integration alone is limited.

3   An Integrative Framework

In order to produce an integrative framework, we need to establish a generic model of
CSCW systems. Some work has already been completed in this area [5], [7] [14],
[15], [18]. A CSCW system may be seen as consisting of an ontological model, a coordination model and a user interface model [4]. We have analysed CSCW systems in
the light of this viewpoint and have developed the following definitions for the three
models. The ontological model specifies all objects in the application, their relationships and terminologies. The co-ordination model specifies how interactions occur
within the system and describes workflow. The user interface model describes how
the users see the system and how the system is presented at an interface level. In a
fully integrated system all three aspects would need to be integrated. Figure 1 shows
different levels of integration from an architectural viewpoint. This is our top level
architectural framework for integration. The ontological, coordination and user interface models together form the conceptual model for the system.

We propose that two further models should form part of the conceptual model.
These are a security model and a transaction model. The security model shows, which
actors have the rights to which objects. This model should work closely with the ontological model. The transaction model, which covers exception handling and helps
maintain the integrity of the system. This model is associated with the coordination
model. For more detail, the reader is referred to [8].

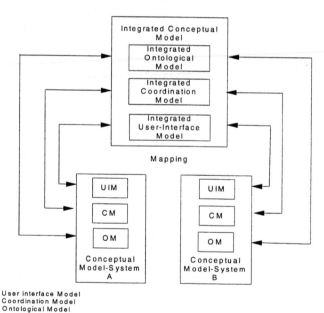

Figure 1: Framework for integration of CSCW

4   An Integrative Model

An application data model represents information that is used for some particular purpose [10], while an integration model has a more generic structure than the models they integrate [9]. The integration model contains some primitive concepts as the building blocks for the definition of other concepts [9], [10]. We use the primitive concepts, which are based on the strengths and commonalities of different models and theories i.e., coordination theory [16], activity theory [15], tasks manager model [14], action/interaction theory [7] and object oriented activity support model [18]. These models and theories have long been established and recognised as an important aid to the development of CSCW applications [5]. The comparison of these concepts is shown in table 2. For more detail, the reader is referred to [5]. We use these concepts as the building blocks of our integration model. These concepts are common to all applications and the advantage is that they are independent of target application [6].

Table 2: Common Terminology [5]

	Activity	Actor	Resource/ Object	Tool
Coordination theory	activity	actor	resource	-----
Activity theory	activity/action	participant , subject	object	tool
Task Manager	task/subtask	person, participant, observer	resource	-----
Action/ Interaction theory	activity/action	member, interactant	-----	technology
OOActSM	activity/ subactivity	actor	document, information	tool

Integration is an activity that creates, modifies, or extends an integration model [9]. Mapping is an activity that creates a map between two applications [10]. Some integration models use an ontology in order to achieve interoperability in heterogeneous applications [1]. In order to build a shared ontology, conflict analysis needs to be carried out. The conflict analysis plays a crucial role in the integration process. This is a well-known problem. According to [2], [11], [12], [13], various relationships between the terminologies can be recognized during the analysis and integration process. The terminology classification and their relationship is described in table 3.

In order to integrate applications, we need to map these applications to each other and to the integrated model. The integrated model contains primitive concepts such as activity, actor, object and tool. They are abstract level concepts. If the application model includes concepts other than those in the integrated model, then the integrated model will be extended.

An integrative model generally supports synchronous and asynchronous activity, which enables a group of people or a virtual team to exchange information and to interact with each other. In a synchronous session, all users share a single view of the discussion and information is exchanged as soon as it is made available. On the other hand, in asynchronous session, information is exchanged only on demand.   The applications which wish to communicate with each other needs to register with the platform. Whenever a new application wants to share information with already existing ones, the platform synchronises the state of the sessions. In this way, the participants applications are supposed to redraw their interfaces.

Table 3: Terminology classification and their relationship

Relationship	Description
Identical concept	Same concept, same meaning and same structure/constraints
Synonyms	Same concept (meaning) but different name
Homonyms	Same name but different meaning
Compatible	Same concept, same meaning and different structure/constraints but not contradictory
In-compatible	Same concept, same meaning and different structure/constraints but contradictory
Complex concept	A group of one or more concepts in one application corresponds to one or more concepts in an integration model
Partitioned concepts	Two or more concepts in one application corresponds to a single general concept in an integration model

5 Integration of applications

This section presents a case study integrating two applications of our university. The first application is document management, an asynchronous collaborative application. This application helps us monitor modules of different disciplines in the university. We will integrate this application with another application namely module assignment. Module assignment is also an asynchronous collaborative application. This application is used to assign different modules to the lecturers. To gain insight into the applications, we have developed the conceptual models of the selected applications. The conceptual models are shown in figure 2 and 3 respectively. We have developed the models according to our experience with these applications.

5.1 Integrative Process

Here, we discuss these applications in terms of their ontology, security, coordination, transaction, and user interface models. Developing a common understanding of existing applications is a pre-requisite to successful integration. In the example we use a generic term actor for lecturer.

The ontological model specifies all objects in the application, and their relationship and terminologies [8]. The document management system offers objects such as 'modules', and 'log book'. The operations on the 'module' are; 'view', 'add', 'delete', 'edit', 'accept' and 'reject' the module. The operation on the 'log book' is; 'view' and 'edit'.

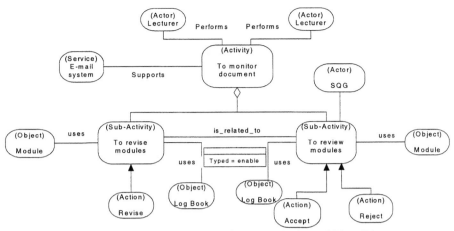

Figure 2: Document Management System—Activity Object Diagram

In the document management system, a part of an actor's work is a sequence of operations on objects such as one actor views a module and then he or she decides to edit it while at the same time he or she views and makes entries in the 'log book'. The administrator performs different operations such as 'add' or 'delete' if he or she wants to add the module in the list or delete the existing module. The Subject Quality Group (SQG) performs different operations. For example, SQG can 'accept' or 'reject' the changes made in the module by the lecturer.

A mapping specification needs to be initiated between applications, which can be procedural, or declarative, or a combination of both. Mapping can be uni-directional or bi-directional. Figure 4 shows the individual ontology. This diagram depicts two ontologies such as ontology p and ontology q. The concept of the 'log book ' has been omitted in the first application for the sake of simplicity.

The (integrative model) mapping between these two applications is shown in figure 5. We have highlighted three concepts according to the primitive concepts such as 'actor', 'object' and 'activity'. An activity is shown as a decision box in our diagram. We use a decision box for representation purposes only.

In ontology p, three actors are involved namely lecturer, administrator and a member of subject quality group and these actors are performing their activities, which include 'revise module', 'monitor module' and 'review module' on the same object 'module' in pre-specified order. In ontology q, two actors are involved namely 'administrator' and 'lecturer'. The actors in ontology q are performing their activities such as 'assign module' and 'view module' respectively. They are performing operations on the same object, which is 'module'. The following relationships have been discovered based on contextual information.

identical
(ontology-p.lecturer) == (ontology-q.lecturer)

identical
(ontology-p.administrator) == (ontology-q.administrator)

identical
(ontology-p.module) == (ontology-q.module)

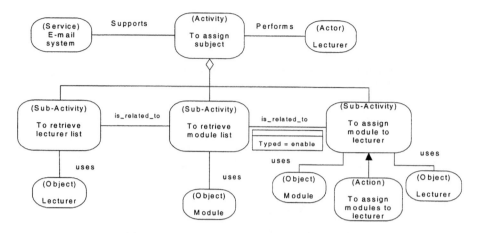

Figure 3: Module Assignment System—Activity Object Diagram

The security model specifies actors/activities and objects and relevant access rights [8]. The security model is related to the ontological model, which provides rights to the actors to access an object or to perform actions on it [4]. For example, one lecturer has a right to access a module, which is to view its contents, and perform some operations on it to modify it. At another moment, the same lecturer may have a right to access the same module, that is to view its contents but he or she is not allowed to make any changes on it. This is a case when the module is being reviewed by SQG. Similarly, in the second application, the security is applied to provide the right to the administrator to access modules, lecturer lists and assign the modules to the lecturers. A lecturer has a right to view the modules allocated to him or her but he or she is not authorised to modify it or to view the modules allocated to other lecturers. In order to integrate the applications, the security measures need to be considered and mapped to each other and to the integrated model.

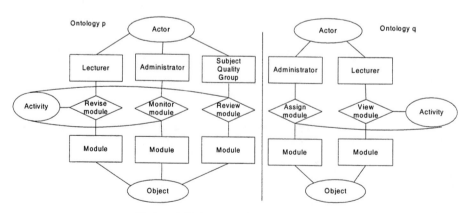

Figure 4: Individual Ontology p and q

48

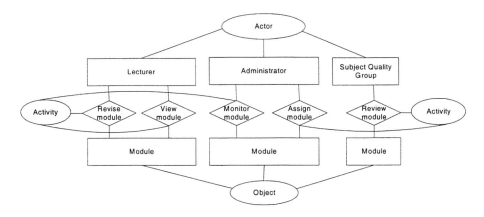

Figure 5: Integrative Model

The coordination model specifies how interactions occur within the system and describes workflow [8]. The main concept of the coordination model is that of an activity [4]. The possible relationships between different classes of objects is seen where revise activity enables review activity. There is a sequence in activities and operations. For example, a lecturer performs operations on a module first, which enables Subject Quality Group (SQG) to review it for quality assurance. Basically, the occurrence of a review activity depends on the occurrence of a revise activity. We consider only the occurrence and non-occurrence of activities in this example.

The levels of coordination can be categorized into two i.e. activity level and object level. An example of the activity level coordination is the fact that a document management system carries out its activities in sequence such as reviewer starts his or her activity using s-action (start action) when revise activity is terminated using t-action (terminate action). While at object level, more than one actor may perform operations on the same object simultaneously. It is managed using locking mechanisms. The transaction model maintains consistency, control, fault tolerance and transparency of distribution at technical level and exception handling, responsibility distribution and work consistency at social level [8].

The user interface model describes how the users see the system and how the system is presented at an interface level [8]. The system presents the objects and operations embodied in the ontological model. The user interface model takes account of different views of objects and the concepts of local operations, which are not available in typical single user applications [4]. Different users may have different views of the same object in one application or in different applications.

The user interface of the first application offers the objects, "modules", and "log book" which are intended for different uses. The module object is displayed on the user's screen in sequence of column and the detail of each module consists of three columns namely serial number, name of the module and code as shown in figure 6a. Once a user selects a module, the contents of the module are displayed on the screen. The activity "revise module" is supposed to contain a replacement text. The system provides an authorised user with operations to replace the original text of the module.

The "log book" object is supposed to contain the reviewers comments. The log book offers every user to make an entry but does not allow replacement.

On the other hand, the user interface of the second application displays the same object module in sequence of rows and the detail of each module consists of three rows namely serial number, name of the module and code for that module as shown in figure 6b. We have designed an integrated interface using model view controller (MVC). This integrated interface provides the facility to the user to select how he or she wants to view the detail of modules such as in a sequence of rows or columns.

The design of MVC separates the application object (model) from the way it is represented to the user (view) and from the way in which the user controls it (controller). It is used to organize the systems, which support multiple presentation of the same information [19]. Space permits some details to be omitted.

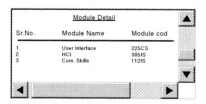
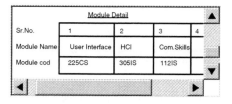

Figure: 6a: Interface of Application 1   Figure 6b: Interface of Application 2

6   Conclusion and Future Work

In this paper, we have discussed the need for open CSCW systems and considered how integration might be achieved in CSCW. To this end we have looked at generic models for CSCW and developed our own model based on previous work. A framework for integration has been presented. The framework has been evaluated using a case study and initial results indicate that the framework appears to be a useful tool for analyzing CSCW systems for integration and interoperability. The work is novel in that no integrative framework for CSCW exists currently. It is envisaged that systems developers would use this framework to support integration work. Our future work will include detailed development and further evaluation of the framework.

Reference

1. Akahani, J., Hiramatsu, K., and Kogure, K., (2002): 'Coordinating heterogeneous information services based on approximate onotology translation', AAMAS-2002 Workshop on Agentcities: Challenges in Open Agent Systems.
2. Batini C., Lenzerini M., and Navathe S.B., C., (1986): 'A comparative analysis of methodologies for database schema integration', ACM Computer Survey, Vol 18, No.4, 323-364.
3. Benford, S., J. Mariani, L.Navarro, W.Prinz and T.Rodden, (1993): 'MOCCA: An Environment for CSCW Applications', ACM Organizational Computing Systems, Milpitas – California, Press, PP.172-77.

4. Ellis, C. and Wainer, J. (1994)'A Conceptual Model of Groupware', ACM Conference on Computer Supported Cooperative Work, 79-88

5. Farias, C. R. G., Pires, L. F., and Sinderen, M. van: (2000):'A Conceptual model for the development of CSCW systems'. Fifth International conference on the design of cooperative systems (COOP 2000), Sophia Antipolis, pp.189-204.

6. Farias, C. R. G., Pires, L. F., and Sinderen, M. van: (2000): 'A systematic approach for component-based software development'. In Proceedings of the Seventh European Concurrent Engineering Conference (ECEC 2000), pp. 127-131.

7. Fitzpatrick, G., Tolone, W.J. and Kaplan, S.: M. (1995) 'Work, Locales and Distributed Social Worlds', Proceedings of the 1995 European Conference on Computer Supported Cooperative Work (ECSCW '95), pp. 1-16.

8. Iqbal, R., James, A., Gatward, R., (2002): 'A Framework for Integration of CSCW', in Proc. CSCWD02, Computer supported cooperative work in design conference, IEEE, Brazil.

9. ISO TC184/SC4/WG10N320, (2000): 'Industrial Automation Systems and Integration', Integration of Industrial data for exchange, access, and sharing.

10. ISO TC184/SC4/WG10N342, (2002): 'Industrial Automation Systems and Integration', Integration of Industrial data for exchange, access, and sharing.

11. Kashyap, V., and Sheth, A., (1999): 'Semantic Similarities between objects in multiple databases;. Management of Heterogenous and Autonomous Database Systems.

12. Kim, W., et. al., (1993) 'On resolving schematic heterogeneity in multidatabase systems',. Distributed and Parallel Databases, 1(3):25 1-277.

13. Kim, W., and Seo., J., (1991.): 'Classifying schematic and data heterogeneity in multidatabase systems'. IEEE Computer, 24(12):12-l.

14. Kreifelts, T., Hinrichs, E. and Woetzel, G.: (1993): 'Sharing To-Do Lists with a Distributed Task Manager', Proceedings of the Third European Conference on Computer Supported Cooperative Work (ECSCW'93), pp. 31-46.

15. Kuutti, K.: (1991): 'The concept of activity as a basic unit of analysis for CSCW research', Proceedings of the Second European Conference on Compute Supported Co-operative Work (ECSCW'91), pp. 249-264.

16. Malone, T. W. and Crowston, K.(1990): 'What is Coordination Theory and how can it help design cooperative work systems' ACM Conference on Computer Supported Cooperative Work (CSCW'90), pp. 357-370.

17. Navarro, L., Prinz, W., and Rodden, T.,(1993): 'CSCW requires Open Systems', Computer Communications, Vol. 16, No. 5, pp. 288-297.

18. Teege, G.: (1996.): 'Object-Oriented Activity Support: A Model for Integrated CSCW Systems. Computer Supported Cooperative Work (CSCW)', The Journal of Collaborative Computing, 5(1), pp. 93-124.

19. Wheeler, S., (1996): Object-Oriented Programming with X-Designer http://atddoc.cern.ch/Atlas/ Notes/004/Note004-1.html.

Implementing Mediators through Virtual Updateable Views[1]

Hanna Kozankiewicz[*], Jacek Leszczyłowski[*], Kazimierz Subieta[*#]

[*]) Institute of Computer Science, Polish Ac.Sci., Warsaw, Poland
[#]) Polish-Japanese Institute of Information Technologies, Warsaw, Poland
{hanka, jacek, subieta}@ipipan.waw.pl

Abstract. Mediators are considered basic architectural units for integration of distributed, heterogeneous information resources. In the paper we propose powerful virtual updateable views as a very high-level tool for their implementation. We assume that a view definer can explicitly determine view updates intention through procedures (being a part of a view definition) which dynamically overload generic view updating operations. We follow the Stack-Based Approach, a new theory of object-oriented query languages based on the classical concepts of programming languages, such as the environment stack and the naming-scoping-binding paradigm. The proposal addresses very general object-oriented model and offers full computational power of a mediator definition language.

1 Introduction

The growth of business-oriented applications of the Internet has caused the necessity to provide mechanisms for integration of distributed and heterogeneous data/service resources. The topic has already been investigated in various contexts, such as federated databases and CORBA-oriented applications. A new term - mediator [Wied92] - has been coined to denote an architectural unit of a such integration. Mediators transform data from one format into another and provide generalization and abstraction over data. They also combine, refine, and integrate data from multiple sources.

An unsolved issue concerning mediators concerns the methodology, tools and rules that can be efficiently used for their design and construction. Till now, this part of the technology seems to be immature. Typically, mediators are implemented in lower level programming languages like C++ or Java. Such an approach has disadvantages - an increased time and cost of development, clumsy and long code, poor reuse, high maintenance cost and time. There are proposals to implement mediators in declarative languages [BRU96]. Following them we claim that mediator functionalities can be provided by means of powerful database virtual views. The use of views to integrate heterogeneous ontologies has already been discussed in [Subi01].

Apart from advantages of database views as tools for implementing mediators there are several difficult problems. We identify them as follows:

---

[1] Supported by the European Commission 5th Framework project ICONS (Intelligent Content Management System); no. IST-2001-32429.

- Computational/algorithmic universality of the view definition language. Standard SQL is not sufficiently universal, hence in many cases it cannot be used to specify mediators.
- Data model and data structures that view definitions address. SQL addresses only relational structures, but majority of Web resources are or will be based on XML-oriented data, or even more complex RDF-oriented, object-oriented or object-relational structures.
- The view updating problem. This concerns mediators that have to update source databases. Current solutions of the problem are limited, despite of intensive research. Limited view updating possibilities reduce applicability of the idea.
- Performance. A mediator should not imply significant performance penalty. This means new needs for optimization of queries involving views.

Views are the subject of many research efforts in the context of XML technologies [Abit00], object-oriented and object-relational databases [ABS97, LaSc91, SLT91]. There are some implemented prototypes like views in O2 [Souz95], ActiveViews [AAC+99], or stored functional procedures in Loqis [Subi91]. View concepts occur also in the ODMG standard [ODMG00] (the "define" statement of OQL) and in the SQL:99 standard [MSG01]. Nevertheless, in our opinion no current proposal concerning views presents satisfactory idea how to cope with the above mentioned problems. This is the motivation of our research, which addresses all of them.

Our idea is simple and straightforward. A view definition is a complex module that consists of not only a single query (as in SQL) but contains a part that allows the view definer to take full control over view updates. The part consists of procedures that dynamically overload generic view updates of virtual objects. The procedures are defined on top of a query language [SKL95]. The view definer should write an appropriate procedure for each of necessary view updating operations. Queries involving such views are optimizable through the query modification technique [SuPl01]. The idea is exactly in the spirit of the *instead of* triggers of Oracle and MS SQL Server, but it is much more general and applicable to non-relational database/web systems.

The approach has obvious consequences:

- Query language must be computationally complete and must address a complex object-oriented model (covering other models - relational, XML, etc.)
- On top of the query language there must be defined imperative statements a la SQL *update*, *insert* and *delete*. Such statements can be involved into control statements such as *if, while, for each*, etc.
- On top of the above there must be defined functions and procedures, with parameters, a la SQL stored procedures (in the style of Oracle PL/SQL).

The above assumptions exclude the traditional approaches to query languages based on relational algebras, calculi, logic and their object-oriented counterparts. The view mechanism presented in this paper is defined within the Stack Based Approach (SBA) to query languages [SKL95]. The approach has roots in the semantics of programming languages. It integrates query languages' and programming languages' concepts into a unified, consistent and non-redundant system of notions. It is abstract and universal, which makes it relevant to a general object model. The approach has already been implemented in a prototype Loqis [Subi91] (an object-oriented DBMS), in a prototype addressing an object model with dynamic object roles [SJHP03], in a prototype of an XML-oriented query language for the DOM model [HP02], and in other prototypes. Currently we are working on a prototype for the EU project ICONS, where all features presented in this paper have to be implemented.

The presented approach meets the requirements included in the report of I^3/POB working group [BRU96] that is devoted to a standard language for mediators: it supports complex data types and for their arbitrary combination, semi-structured data, abstract data types (as a particular case of the class concept), and other required features.

The rest of this paper is structured as follows. In the next section we formalize data store structures. Section 3 introduces the notion of an environment stack and describes its main roles i.e. name scoping and binding. Section 4 presents the Stack Based Query Language (SBQL). Section 5 introduces our approach to updateable views and Section 6 presents examples illustrating its power. Section 7 concludes.

2 Abstract Object Store Model

In order to formalize a language for view/mediator specification we have to formalize data structures that it addresses. In the paper we focus on simple data stores, which contain nested objects and relationships between them. We would like to emphasize that in SBA the store model and its query language can be easily extended to very complex object models, including notions of classes, inheritance, and dynamic roles (see [SJHP03]).

In SBA each object consists of the following components:
- Internal identifier (OID) that is automatically assigned and identifies the object.
- External name (introduced by a designer, programmer or user) used to access the object from a query or program.
- Content that can be a value, a link, or a set of objects.

Let I be a set of the internal identifiers, N be a set of the external names, and V be a set of the atomic values, e.g. numbers, strings, blobs, etc. Atomic values include also codes of procedures, functions, methods, views, and other procedural entities. Formally objects are modeled as triples defined below, where i, i_1, $i_2 \in I$, $n \in N$, and $v \in V$:
- Atomic objects *as* <i, n, v>.
- Link objects *as* $<i_1, n, i_2>$. that model relationships between objects.
- Complex objects *as* <i, n, S>, where S denotes a set of objects.

Note that this definition is recursive and allows one to create linked and compound objects with an arbitrary number of hierarchy levels. To model collections SBA does not impose uniqueness of external names at any level of data hierarchy (as in XML). In SBA, objects populate an object store, which consists of the following elements:
- The structure of objects, subobjects, etc.
- OIDs of root objects, which are accessible from the outside (starting points for querying).
- Constraints (e.g. uniqueness of OIDs, referential integrities, etc).

Example data store. A schema of the store presented in Fig.1 describes a part of a database for a bookstore. Fig.1 also contains a sample state of the object store.

54

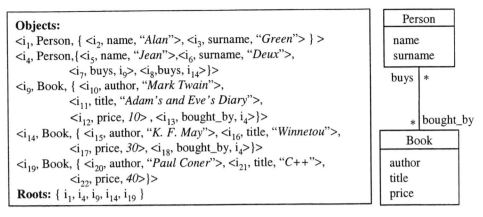

Objects:
<i_1, Person, { <i_2, name, *"Alan"*>, <i_3, surname, *"Green"*> } >
<i_4, Person,{<i_5, name, *"Jean"*>,<i_6, surname, *"Deux"*>,
           <i_7, buys, i_9>, <i_8,buys, i_{14}>}>
<i_9, Book, { <i_{10}, author, *"Mark Twain"*>,
           <i_{11}, title, *"Adam's and Eve's Diary"*>,
           <i_{12}, price, *10*> , <i_{13}, bought_by, i_4>}>
<i_{14}, Book, { <i_{15}, author, *"K. F. May"*>, <i_{16}, title, *"Winnetou"*>,
           <i_{17}, price, *30*>, <i_{18}, bought_by, i_4>}>
<i_{19}, Book, { <i_{20}, author, *"Paul Coner"*>, <i_{21}, title, *"C++"*>,
           <i_{22}, price, *40*>}>
Roots: { i_1, i_4, i_9, i_{14}, i_{19} }

Person
name
surname
buys *

Book
author
title
price

* bought_by

Fig. 1. The example object store and its schema

3 Name Binding

The foundation of SBA is the naming-scoping-binding mechanism, which ensures that each name occurring in a query is bound to an appropriate run-time entity (an object, attribute, method, parameter, etc.) according to the scope of this name. Scope control and name binding is managed using an environment stack (ES) – a structure well-known in programming languages. The stack enables the *abstraction principle*, which allows the programmer to consider the currently being written piece of code to be independent of the contexts of its possible uses.

ES consists of *sections* that contain sets of *binders*. A binder is an SBA concept used to cope with various naming issues that occur in object models and their query languages. Formally, a binder is a pair (n, x), where n is an external name, and x is a reference to an object; such a pair is written as $n(x)$. We refer to n as the *binder name*, and to x as its *binder value*. The concept of a binder is generalized; in particular, x can be an atomic value or a compound structure.

In SBA, at the beginning of a user session ES consists of base sections containing binders for all root database objects. Usually there exist other base sections with binders to computer environment variables, to local objects of the user session, to libraries, etc. During query evaluation the stack grows and shrinks according to query nesting. Assuming there are no side effects in queries (no calls of updating methods), the final ES state is exactly the same as the initial one.

The process which determines the meaning of an external name is called *binding*. Binding follows the "search from the top" rule: to bind a name n the binding mechanism is looking for the ES "visible" section closest to the top of the stack and containing a binder having the considered name n. If the binder is $n(x)$ then the result of the binding is x. To cover collections, SBA allows that the binding can be multi-valued, that is, if the relevant section contains several binders whose names are n: $n(x_1)$, $n(x_2)$, $n(x_3)$,..., then all of them contribute to the result of the binding. In such a case the binding of n returns the collection $\{x_1, x_2, x_3, ...\}$. Fig.2 presents an example ES with base section containing binders to root objects of the store showed in Fig.1 and with one additional section at the top containing binders representing the content of the object i_4. Arrows indicate the order of name binding search.

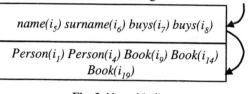

Fig. 2. Name binding

Function nested. Function nested allows constructing new section(s) on the top of ES. For an element r the function returns a set of binders in the following way:

- If r is a single identifier of a complex object, e.g. i_4, then *nested* returns binders to subobjects of given object (in Fig.2 the top section of the stack contains the internal environment of $Person(i_4)$).
- If r is an identifier of a link object, e.g., i_7, then *nested* returns binders to the object the link points to (e.g. for i_7 it is $\{Book(i_9)\}$).
- If r is a binder, then *nested* returns $\{r\}$ (a set consisting of the binder).
- If r is a structure $struct\{r_1, r_2, r_3, ...\}$, then *nested* returns the sum of results returned by *nested* for $r_1, r_2, r_3, ...$
- For other r *nested* returns the empty set.

4 Stack Based Query Language (SBQL)

SBQL [SKL95] is a formalized query language in the spirit of OQL. Its syntax is:

- A single name or a single literal is an (atomic) query. For instance, *Person, name, y*, "Smith", 2500, etc, are queries. Note that the identifiers are not representable.
- If q is a query, and σ is a unary operator (e.g. sum, count, distinct, sin, sqrt), then $\sigma(q)$ is a query.
- If q_1 and q_2 are queries, and θ is a binary operator (e.g. *where, dot, join*, =, *and*), then $q_1 \, \theta \, q_2$ is a query.

SBQL is based on the principle of operator orthogonality, which means that operators can be freely combined unless it violates some type constraints. We distinguish algebraic and non-algebraic operators – the subdivision is explained below.

Query Results. We denote the set of results of SBQL queries *Result* and elements of this set *q_values*. SBQL queries can only return one of the following *q_value*:

- atomic value (e.g. 3, 'Smith', TRUE, etc.)
- reference to an object (of any kind, e.g. i_1, i_5, i_8, i_{18}.)
- binder n(v), where v is a *q_value* and n is any name.
- structure $struct\{v_1, v_2, v_3, ...\}$ where $v_1, v_2, v_3, ...$ are *q_values* and *struct* is a structure constructor. In general, an order of elements is essential. This constraint can be relaxed providing all v_i are binders. This construct generalizes a tuple known from the relational model.

- collections: $bag\{$ v_1, v_2, v_3,,... $\}$, $sequence$ $\{$ v_1, v_2, v_3, ... $\}$, ... where bag, $sequence$, ... are collection constructors, and v_1, v_2, v_3, ... are q_values.

Algebraic operators. The operator is algebraic if its semantics is expressed without involving ES. Algebraic operators include numerical, string and boolean comparisons and operators, aggregate functions, set, bag and sequence comparisons and operators , the Cartesian product, etc. Let q_1 and q_2 be queries and Δ be a symbol denoting a binary algebraic operator Δ. Then, in order to evaluate the query $q_1 \Delta q_2$, queries q_1 and q_2 are evaluated independently and then Δ is performed on two partial results (taking them in the proper order), returning the final result.

Non-algebraic operators. Non-algebraic operators are defined in terms of ES. They include selection, projection/navigation, dependent join, quantifiers, and others. We have rejected the common view that these operators can be "algebralized" in the relational algebra style. This can be done only by shifting a part of the semantics to the informal meta-language of mathematics, and we would like definitely to avoid that. If the query $q_1 \theta q_2$ involves a non-algebraic operator θ, then q_2 is evaluated in the context determined by q_1. Thus, the order of evaluation of sub-queries q_1 and q_2 is significant. These operators are called "non-algebraic" because they do not follow the basic property of algebraic expressions, i.e. independent evaluation of q_1 and q_2.

The query $q_1 \theta q_2$ is evaluated as follows. For each element r of q_value returned by q_1, the subquery q_2 is evaluated. Before such an evaluation, a new section $nested(r)$ is pushed on ES. After the evaluation ES returns to the previous state. A partial result of the evaluation is a combination of r and the q_value returned by q_2 for that r; the combination depends on θ. Partial results are merged into the final result.

Procedures. SBQL incorporates procedures, with or without parameters, returning an output or not. A procedure parameter can be any query. We adopt *call-by-value, call-by-reference* and other parameter passing methods. There are no limitations on computational complexity, what can be useful for view definitions when the mapping between stored and imaginary objects is complex and requires non-trivial algorithms. The results of functional procedures (functions) belong to the same semantic category as results of queries, therefore they can be invoked in queries. Due to ES, there are no restrictions on calling functions within the body of (other) functions, what enables among others recursive calls. So far SBQL and the procedures are untyped, but another research group intends to introduce static type checking.

Below, we present an example function *bestsellers* returning books which were sold in more then *nb_sold* pieces; *nb_sold* is a *call-by-value* function parameter:

```
function bestsellers ( in nb_sold ) {
    return Book where count ( bought_by ) > nb_sold; }
```

A call of this function is shown in a query:

```
Get authors and titles of books that were sold in more then 500 pieces:
    bestsellers( 500 ) . (title, author)
```

5 Updateable Views

In majority of the classical approaches (relational, object-relational and object-oriented) a database view is essentially a functional procedure. View updates are performed through side effects of view definitions, usually through various kinds of references to stored data returned by view invocations. The art of view updating focuses on forbidding updates that may violate user intention, c.f. view updateability criteria, such as no view over-updating.

We abandon this approach and disallow any updates through side effects. Instead, we explicitly introduce information on intents of view updates in the form of procedures that overload generic view updating operations. Our approach to updateable views is described in detail in [KLPS02]. We propose a two-query paradigm to operations on views. The first query preserves all the necessary information about the stored source objects involved in the view, while the second query takes the result of the first query as an input and delivers the final mapping between stored and virtual objects. The first part in the two-query paradigm is a *sack definition*. A sack contains *seeds*, which unambiguously identify stored objects, which "induce" the virtual ones. A seed is a parameter of updating procedures defined by the view definer for determining view updates. This parameter is passed implicitly (it is internal to the proposed mechanism) and the view definer does not need to bother about it.

We distinguished the following operations on virtual objects:

- deletion of a given object.
- insertion of a new object inside a given object (inserted object's id is a parameter).
- dereferencing that returns the value of an object.
- updating the value of a given object. The operation has a new value as a parameter.

A view definer has to write an overloading procedure for each operation that he/she wish to support. If some overloading procedure is not defined, then the corresponding operation is not supported (it is forbidden). We ascribed fixed procedure names (*on_delete*, *on_insert*, *on_retrieve*, *on_update*) to these operations, which have a different syntactic representation in a programming language. Names of formal parameters of procedures *on_insert* and *on_update* can be chosen by the view definer. We provide a typical method of passing parameters to procedures bodies through binders inserted into a corresponding ES activation record.

View definition can also include definition of sub-views. Our idea is based on the *relativity principle*, which assumes that each nested entity has the same syntactic and semantic properties as the external one. Hence sub-views are defined in the same way.

We can define a view *ClientDef* with information about persons who have ever bought a book in our bookstore. We define operation of dereference returning client name and we allow deletion of the client. The view definition may looks as follows:

```
create view ClientDef {
    virtual objects Client {(Person where count( buys ) > 0) as c;}
    on_retrieve do { return c . name; }
    on_delete do { delete c; }}
```

We distinguish in a uniform way the view definition name from the name of virtual objects generated by the view. In the example we use names *ClientDef* (required for view creating, updating, and deleting) and *Client* (that identifies virtual objects).

View definitions are kept in an object store. An ES database section has to contain both: a binder to the view definition (required to use/change the view's definition) and a binder to the sack definition (that allows querying/updating virtual objects). Observe, that this allows the separation of a view definition from existence of virtual objects. Thus it is possible to have a view defined in some place and not "activated" – with no virtual objects existing. Besides, one may have virtual objects derived according to the same view definition several times and in each of the times they may exist in a different place.

View Call Processing. View call processing requires passing of information on virtual objects to the proper updating procedure defined within the view. The system has to determine whether it deals with a stored or virtual object, which view, and which virtual object. Therefore, we have introduced a *virtual identifier* of the form:

<Flag "I am virtual", View definition identifier, Seed>

When a system processes a virtual identifier it pushes on ES a section containing *nested(seed)* and a section with binders to all sub-views definitions of the processed view. In such a way we pass the *seed* parameter to all the (dereferencing, updating) procedures that and make all subviews (i.e. attributes of virtual objects) available for querying.

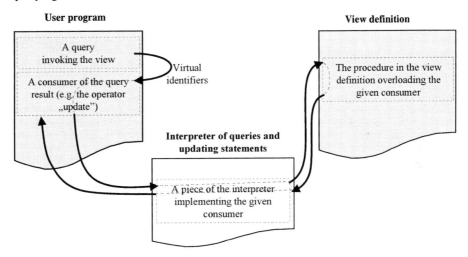

Fig. 3. Processing of a view call.

In Fig.3 we depicted a flow of control during processing a view update operation. First, the query involving a view is evaluated and it returns virtual identifier(s). A user program determines which operation should be performed and passes the control to the query interpreter. It recognizes that the operation concerns a virtual object and passes control to a proper procedure from the proper view definition. When the procedure execution is finished, the control returns to the user program.

Views with Parameters and Recursive Views. Views, similarly to procedures, can have parameters. A parameter can be any query - in particular, it may return a bag $bag(r_1, r_2, ..., r_n)$ where $r_1, r_2, ..., r_n \in Result$. A query interpreter determines a method of parameters passing basing on the view definition syntax. We are going to implement a method known as *strict-call-by-value*, in which the result of a query being a parameter is passed without any change to the procedure's body. Technically, it means that if for a formal parameter *par* the query returns a result *r*, then to the corresponding activation record for procedure *p* is added a single binder *par(r)*. In this way the result of the query becomes available within the *p* body under the name *par*. Currently, in our approach parameters concern only seed definitions and are not available for definitions of updating procedures (it is possible, but requires small extensions of the mechanism).

Recursion is given for free within the stack-based semantics. As shown, views are programming entities like functions and procedures. All volatile data created by the view are pushed on ES, thus each view call is independent on other view calls. Hence, recursive views are fully supported by the described mechanism

Nested views. For nesting views we have to extend the notion of virtual identifiers for virtual objects from subviews to enable access to all seeds of parent virtual objects along the path of nesting. A possible extended form of a virtual identifier is:

<Flag "I am virtual", (View definition identifier₁, Seed₁),
..., (View definition identifierₙ, Seedₙ) >

where (*View definition identifier₁, Seed₁*) refers to the most outer view, and (*View definition identifierₙ, Seedₙ*) refers to the current inner view.

When an identifier is processed by any of the procedures *on_retrieve*, *on_update*, *on_delete*, or *on_insert*, the interpreter pushes on ES a section containing *nested(Seed₁)* $\cup$ *nested(Seed₂)* $\cup$ ... $\cup$ *nested(Seedₙ)*, and then calls the proper procedure. This is the way of passing information on seeds to all the procedures.

6 View Examples

In this section we present examples illustrating power of the approach. In the examples we use the database presented in Fig.1.

Currency conversion. We define a view that for each book returns a virtual object containing book's title and its price in Euro (we assume that prices are kept in the database in USD). The view defines an operation of a price rise, where an amount of rise is given in Euro (the corresponding procedure transforms it in USD and raises the price). The view definition looks as follows:

```
create view BookTitleEuroPriceDef {
    virtual objects BookTitleEuroPrice{ return Book as b; }

    create view BookTitleDef {
        virtual objects BookTitle { return b.title as bt; }
        on_retrieve do { return bt; }   }
```

```
create view EuroPriceDef {
    virtual objects EuroPrice { return b.price as bp; }
    on_retrieve do { return bp * CurrentDollarToEuroExchangeRate(); }
    on_update new_euro_price do {
        if new_euro_price < 0 then { print("Error: New book price < 0?"); return;}
        else bp := new_euro_price /CurrentDollarToEuroExchangeRate(); } } }
```

Call of the view in a query that decreases the price of the "Winnetou" book on 10 Euro:

```
for each BookTitleEuroPrice where BookTitle = "Winnetou" do
        EuroPrice:= EuroPrice - 10;
```

Providing security. We define a view returning information on clients and books they have bought in a bookstore. The information about books is public, unlike information about clients that should be available only for authorized users. The view should protect these data against hackers by returning false results instead of forbidding access. The example is under influence of [SJGP90].

```
create view BooksClientInfoDef {
    virtual objects BooksClientInfo { return Book as b;}
    on_retrieve do { return b; }

    create view ClientDef {
        virtual objects Client { return b.bought_by.Person.surname as c;}
        on_retrieve do {
            if AccessIsAuthorised() then return c;
            else {
                create local FalseClients := sequence {"Smith", "White", "Black"};
                return selectRandomCombinationOf( FalseClients );        } } } }
```

7 Summary

We have presented an approach to implementing mediators through very powerful object-oriented updateable views. The mechanism is based on the Stack Based Approach to query languages. We have shown that the presented approach allows one to define very powerful views in which the view definer has full control over what happens with updates of virtual objects. We provide using such views to integrate heterogeneous data resources in federated database and/or web systems.

Our future work on the presented view mechanism, after finishing the implementation for an XML-oriented store, will focus on extending the concept on more complex data stores and on introducing new extensions to the view mechanism e.g. introducing stateful views, classes for virtual objects, etc. which could be very useful in the context of mediators.

References

[AAC+99] S.Abiteboul, B.Amman, S.Cluet, A.Eyal, L.Mignet, T.Milo. Active Views for Electronic Commerce. Proc. of VLDB Conf., 1999, 138-149.

[Abit00] S.Abiteboul. On Views and XML. Proc. of PODS Conf., 1999, 1-9

[ABS97] S.Amer-Yahia, P. Breche, and C. Souza dos Santos. Objects Views and Updates. Engineering of Information Systems Journal 5(1), 1997.

[BRU96] P.Buneman, L.Rashid, J.Ullman. Mediator Languages - a Proposal for a Standard. Report of an I3/POB Working Group, University of Maryland, April 1996

[HP02] R.Hryniów, T.Pieciukiewicz. A Stack-Based XML Query Language. Master's thesis, Polish-Japanese Institute of Information Technology, 2002.

[KLPS02] H.Kozankiewicz, J.Leszczyłowski, J.Płodzień, and K.Subieta. Updatable Object Views. Institute of Computer Science, Polish Ac.Sci, Report 950, 2002

[LaSc91] C.Laasch, M.H.Scholl, M.Tresch. Updatable Views in Object-Oriented Databases. Proc. of 2nd DOOD Conf., Springer LNCS 566, 1991

[MSG01] J.Melton, A.R.Simon, J.Gray. SQL:1999 - Understanding Relational Language Components. Morgan Kaufmann Publishers, 2001

[ODMG00] Object Data Management Group: The Object Database Standard ODMG, Release 3.0. R.G.G.Cattel, D.K.Barry, Ed., Morgan Kaufmann, 2000

[SJGP90] M.Stonebraker, A.Jhingran, J.Goh, S.Potamianos: On Rules, Procedures, Caching and Views in Data Base Systems. Proc. of SIGMOD Conf., 1990, 281-290

[SJHP03] K.Subieta, A.Jodłowski, P.Habela, J.Płodzień. Conceptual Modeling of Business Applications with Dynamic Object Roles. (in) "Technologies Supporting Business Solutions", The ACTP Series, Nova Science Books and Journals, USA, 2003

[SKL95] K.Subieta, Y.Kambayashi, J.Leszczylowski. Procedures in Object-Oriented Query Languages. VLDB 1995: 182-193

[SLT91] M.H.Scholl, C.Laasch, M.Tresch. Updatable Views in Object-Oriented Databases. Proc. 2-nd DOOD Conf. Springer LNCS 566, 1991

[Souz95] C.Souza dos Santos. Design and Implementation of Object-Oriented Views, Proc. of DEXA Conf., Springer LNCS 978, 1995, 91-102

[Subi01] K.Subieta. Mapping Heterogeneous Ontologies Through Object Views. EFIS'01

[Subi91] K.Subieta. LOQIS: The Object-Oriented Database Programming System. Proc. 1st Intl. East/West Database Workshop on Next Generation Information System Technology, Springer LNCS 504, 1991, 403-421

[SuPl01] K.Subieta, J.Płodzień. Object Views and Query Modification, (in) "Databases and Information Systems", Kluwer Academic Publishers, pp. 3-14, 2001

[Wied92] G.Wiederhold. Mediators in the Architecture of Future Information Systems, IEEE Computer Magazine, March 1992

Schema Integration on Federated Spatial DB across Ontologies

Villie Morocho[1], Fèlix Saltor[1], and Lluís Pérez-Vidal[2]

[1] Departament de LSI-SI, Universitat Politècnica de Catalunya,
Jordi Girona 1-3,08034. Barcelona, Spain.
`{vmorocho,saltor}@lsi.upc.es`
[2] Departament de LSI-IG, Universitat Politècnica de Catalunya,
Av. Diagonal ,647 08028. Barcelona, Spain.
`lpv@lsi.upc.es`

Abstract. Information integration has been an important area of research for many years, and the problem of integration of geographic data has recently emerged. This paper presents an approach based on the use of Ontologies for solving the problem of semantic heterogeneity in the process of the construction of a *Federated Schema* in the framework of geographic data. We make use of standard technologies (abstract model and GML from OpenGIS, XMI based XML, SDTS from USGS). The principal ontology for the matching process is derived from Spatial Data Transfer Standard and WordNet. To obtain similarities and differences between entities from *Export Schema*, this work makes use of a semantic similarity model. The notion of context is also an important issue for the evaluation of semantic similarity. The main goal achieved in this work is the use of a Federated Architecture for Spatial Databases in conjunction with the assessment of semantic similarity across ontologies.

1 Introduction

Interoperability and integration of heterogeneous data have been some of the goals to achieve during the last few years. From software corporations to world scientific institutions, researchers are working on it. This paper presents a framework based on BLOOM [1] which is based on Federated Database Architecture [29]. The BLOOM architecture is focused on adding security levels. In one part of this paper we change the scope from traditional DBs to spatial DBs. Inside of this Federated Architecture, at the level of schema integration, we make use of Ontologies for solving Semantic Heterogeneity.

Semantically rich information (i.e. metadata, context information) is added to the *Native Schema* at the bottom level and this information will help in assessing semantic similarity across ontologies in order to allow the construction of the *Federated Schema*. In this framework, after the *Geospatial Schema* level, (in which all models are native), these schemas are transformed into a Canonical Data Model. A Canonical Data Model [8] is a common model for all *Component Schemas*. We make use of the abstract model from OpenGIS Consortium [26] as Canonical Data Model CDM.

The other part of this paper, proposes to materialize the CDM in XMI [25]. The main purpose of XMI is to enable easy interchange of metadata between modeling tools (based on the OMG-UML [24]) and metadata repositories(OMG-MOF based), in a distributed and heterogeneous environment. Once the model in XMI is materialized, we construct the Ontologies for the objects in the model. Then each object should search its equivalence in the WordNet-SDTS [21], [34] ontology and, afterwards, a process of assessing semantic similarity will produce a *Federated Schema*. In this matching process, it is possible to know whether there is a correspondence between Objects, and which is semantically parallel to another. In this way, it is possible to achieve a *semiautomatic* schema integration.

Proceeding with levels of the framework, the Federated Schema should be authorized at the *Authorized Schema* level. After this, it should also be filtered through the *External Schema* to finally obtain a *User Schema* at the top of the framework. The use of ontologies to assist in solving semantic heterogeneities in the integration of federated database is not novel. However, the framework is tackling the particular domain of GIS and spatial data integration and it is exploiting common models to assist in the integration. Especially, the framework takes advantage of additional information present in GISs v.g. , attribute and entity metadata, and others. Therefore, the ontologies can be more accurate at the time of defining the semantic meaning of an object to be assessed. In this paper we first present related works in section 2. We present our architecture in section 3 and then study the use of the abstract model from OpenGIS, GML and XMI in it. Also in section 3.3 we explain how to use ontologies for assessing semantic similarity [28]. Finally, we consider future work and conclusions in the last section.

2   Related works

Schema Integration refers to integration of schemas into a single schema (e.g., federated schema development by integrating schemas in a bottom-up FDBS development process). Many approaches and techniques for schema integration have been reported in the literature. Sheth and Larson in [29] remark the unfeasibility of the complete automatic schema integration process. One of the main problems is the comparison step (identifying naming conflicts, homonyms, or synonyms). From the point of view of integration of spatial databases there is a slight advantage to resolve this problem. Now there is a lot of information available to add as semantic information for schema integration. With the arrival of new technology and new possibilities of storage, it is possible to talk of near automatic solving of semantic heterogeneity in the schema integration process.

Around this approach there are a lot of approximations. Tools developed to perform schema integration are reported in [13], [30], [27]. Recently the focus has changed from schematic to semantic integration of heterogeneous sources [31]. Many approaches for solving semantic problems are considering the use of ontologies as the best solution. Examples are: OBSERVER [19], applies ontologies to replace terms in user queries with suitable terms in target ontologies; SHOE [14] and Ontobroker [2] are in the framework of the semantic Web. They use ontologies to improve the searching abilities on the web. DB-MAIN [33] is a CASE tool. It tries to integrate all the aspects of the Federated Information System development, but in the process of solving semantics for the integration, much intervention of an expert is necessary. CUPID [18] discovers mappings between schema elements extracting information from XML messages and based on their names, data types, constraints and schema structure. Although the CUPID approach has similarities to the present work, the main difference is the use of geographical data models. In this case, the integration problem deals with shape, multi-resolution, multi-representation, and other atributes of the model.

2.1 Ontologies in Geographic Information Systems

Ontologies define semantics independently of data representation and reflect the relevance of data without accessing them. Such a high-level description of the semantics of geographic information will provide more and new means for comparing and integrating spatial data. Also, ontologies enable knowledge reuse by semantically describing data, and may be the result from consensus reached by different GIS communities.

Research approaches for semantic integration from the point of view of spatial and geographic sources are [28], [12], [11]. [28] is based on a subset of two ontologies. Unlike OBSERVER, the solution does not create new ontologies, but creates links between similar entities in distinct ontologies. Fonseca in [12] directs the research from ontologies but not from database schemas. In our research, we profit from the power of ontologies for solving semantic problems in the construction of the federated schema. In those works he identifies "roles" for the different point of view of geospatial information communities GIC, according to their conceptualizations of the world. From the Federated Architecture we consider different federated schemas for different GIC. Hence, we can use the definition of a GIC as a group of users that share an ontology.

3 Federated Architecture with Ontologies

In this section we present our framework proposal for the use of Ontologies inside a Federated Architecture in order to resolve the semantic heterogeneity problem in the schema integration. In Fig.1 we present the framework.

3.1 A Canonical Data Model for Spatial Database

Users had to retain existing GIS internal structures to store spatial phenomena. Thereby, the modeling process did not offer mechanisms that would allow for the representation of reality according to the user's mental model. There are particular characteristics of geographic data that make modeling more complex than in the case of conventional applications. Modeling the spatial aspects is fundamentally important in the creation of geographic databases, mainly because it deals with an abstraction of geographic reality where the user's view of the real world varies. Thereby, the modeling of geographic data requires models which are more specific and capable of capturing the semantics of geographic data, offering higher abstraction mechanisms and implementation independence. Within this geographic context, concepts such as geometry and topology are important in the determination of spatial relationship between objects. From the point of view of Federated Information Systems it is necessary to find a Canonical Data Model capable of representing all schemas with minimum loss of information from the Native Data Model. In [5], [32] present the requirements for a geographic data model. Between the main requirements are multi-representation and multi-resolution of spatial and geographic information [32] In [22] the possibility of OMT-G [5] and model from OpenGIS as CDM was studied. We use the model from OpenGIS Consortium OGC [26] as "Canonical Data Model". allow for the representation of geographic data. This International Standard (also draft of ISO/DIS 19107) specifies conceptual schemas for describing the spatial characteristics of geographic features, and a set of spatial operations consistent with these schemas. It treats vector geometry and topology up to 3 dimensions. In this model it is possible to represent: geometric primitives, geometric complexes, topological complexes and topological complexes with geometric realization. Also, it is possible to represent 0-, 1-, 2- and 3- dimensional objects. And depending of the functional complexity there are: data types only, simple operations, and complete operations. The Geography Markup Language (GML) is an XML encoding for the transport and storage of geographic information. The main GIS commercial packages are compliant with the specifications of GML (ESRI, MapINFO, ORACLE, Galdos and more). Thereby, we think that any solution which GML is part of, will be the most capable to achieve the objective of searching "Interoperability and integration of spatial source". In GML the problem of multi-resolution and multi-representation is dealt with by using some application schema, or style XSLT(eXtensible Stylesheet Language Transformations [36]). This allows the creation of many versions of a set of spatial or geographic data. GML has been designed to uphold the principle of separating

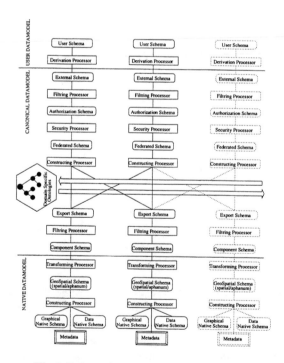

Fig. 1. Federated Architecture with Ontologies

content from presentation. GML provides mechanisms for the encoding of geographic feature data without considering how the data may be presented to a human reader. Since GML is an XML application, it can be readily styled into a variety of presentation formats, including vector and raster graphics, text, sound and voice. Generation of graphical output such as maps is one of the most common presentations of GML, and this can be accomplished in a variety of ways including direct rendering by graphical applets or styling into an XML graphic technology.

3.2 XMI for Codifying the Model

From the GML representation of geographic data, it is possible to obtain the model in XMI representation. The main purpose of XML Metadata Interchange XMI [25] is to enable easy interchange of metadata between modeling tools(based on the OMG-UML[24]) and metadata repositories (OMG-MOF based) in distributed heterogeneous environments. XMI allows metadata to be interchanged as streams of files with a standard XML-based format. The XMI specification supports the interchange of any kind of metadata that can be expressed using the MOF specification, including both model and metamodel information. The specification supports an encoding of metadata consisting of both, a complete model and a model fragment, as well as a tool-specific extension metadata. We propose a representation of the CDM by means of XMI, and obtain a materialized model capable of being parsed. From there it is possible to obtain the Ontologies for each object of the model.

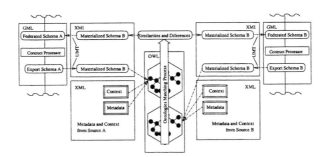

Fig. 2. Creating Ontologies from GML Schemas

The UML Model Transformation Tool, UMT [23] is capable of transforming some XMI into GML and the opposite. In Fig. 2 we present a framework working with this technology. From here, we can make use of UMT as a tool for coding and decoding the GML model, in order to obtain the XMI model and transform it into GML, as well as for the reverse step (to obtain the GML from XMI).

The OWL Web Ontology Language [35] is being designed by the W3C Web Ontology Working Group in order to provide a language that can be used for applications that need to understand the content of information instead of just understanding the human-readable presentation of the content. OWL facilitates a greater machine readability of web content than XML, RDF, and RDF-S support by providing an additional vocabulary for term descriptions. Thereby, it is possible to create metadata, context information and Ontologies from schemas represented in XMI, because all of them are using XML technology. We propose the use of OWL to express the Ontologies and to use the matching techniques [16], [28] for searching similarities and differences between the objects that have to be integrated.

3.3 Constructing the ontologies

The most general approach to semantic integration has been to map the local objects in a database onto a shared ontology [4], [7]. Many efforts that create the shared ontology define a knowledge base in terms of global and domain-independent ontology, e.g. Cyc [17], WordNet [21]. A shared ontology ensures complete integration, but this type of ontology is costly and perhaps impractical, because the maintenance is very complex. In our case, we have limited our work to the GIS domain because there are a lot of standards used for the representation of spatial information [34], [10]. Therefore, there is a lot of information for the creation of ontology depending on the sub-domain in the GIS domain.

In environments with multiple and independent information systems, each system may have its own conceptualization. Different intended models result in multiple domain-dependent ontologies, e.g. medical ontology [37] and engineering ontology [6]. The integration of well defined ontologies may reduce the cost rather than building a global ontology from scratch [20], [15], [3]. But, ontology integration is a complex task. The definition of a systematic and consistent methodology for this integration is a big challenge yet.

In [28] an ontology derived from WordNet [9] and SDTS was constructed. We follow those directives and construct the ontology for the different objects of a schema for the construction of our ontology for assessing semantic similarity of objects from the Export Schema. We extract the names from XMI model by means of parser. Then the matching is divided in two phases:

- *Stage One*: Search of elements from both the user application schema and the database schema onto global ontology.
  - A syntactic search for entity name .
  - A syntactic search for entity parts, attributes names. The ontology elements have parts like in WordNet [21].
  - A semantic search for entity metadata by means of keywords.
  - A semantic search for attributes metadata by means of keywords.

  This result is stored as a first matching reference. It is possible to give a weight for each search and decide if the entity has a corresponding element in the ontology.
- *Stage Two*: Each object from the user application schema will search the corresponding object in the database schema.
  - Assessment of semantic similarity is carried out with a similarity function like the computational model for semantic similarity used in [28]. Taking each entity name from the user schema and comparing against all entity names from the database schema.

- With elements that accept similarity, make the syntactical and semantical comparison between the parts of US entity with the parts of the DBS entity. After this, perform the similarity assessment among entities and attributes metadata. The assessment delivers a set of possible couples. Only the highest assessment will be accepted.
- Whole mapping information is stored in Data/Dictionary/Directory [29]

To demonstrate our approach, we introduce an example of integration of spatial data from different spatial databases and GIS. Our scenario is a compound of two different schemas from a spatial database with geographic information. In both of them there is a class in the Export Schema that represents a "Building area". In **SchemaA** there is a *Building* and in **SchemaB** there is a *Construction*. Both of them have as a property the *Building.Surface* and *Construction.Area*, respectively. *Building* has a relationship with *City* and *Construction* with *Town*. All of them have a geometry inherited Geometry feature from *AbstractGeometry*. In our example we try to obtain a federated schema **SchemaC**, like that in the Fig.3. We will consider that all the models belong to the same GIC.

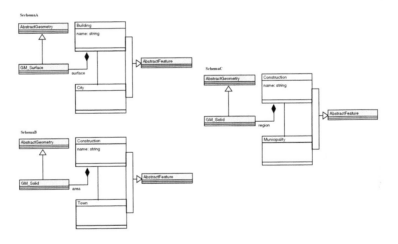

Fig. 3. Federated Schema *SchemaC* from Export Schema *SchemaA, SchemaB*

[28] presents a Matching-Distance Model to compare components of entity classes in terms of a matching process. We can apply this model to solve our problem. First, to obtain the objects for **SchemaC**, we assess the semantic similarity between two objects to integrate. In this case between *Building* and *Construction*. For this assessment we use WordNet-SDTS Ontology, Fig.4, and apply equation 1. The global similarity function $S(c_1, c_2)$ is a weighted sum of the similarity values for parts, functions, and attributes; where ω_p, ω_f, and ω_a are weights of the similarity values for parts, functions, and attributes, respectively. For the complete description of equations refer to [28].

$$S(c_1, c_2) = \omega_p \cdot S_p(c_1, c_2) + \omega_f \cdot S_f(c_1, c_2) + \omega_a \cdot S_a(c_1, c_2) \qquad (1)$$

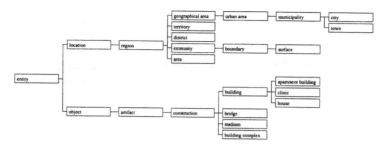

Fig. 4. Partial ontology derived from WordNet and SDTS

We put a limit to accept the similarity. If the similarity is acceptable then we can search the *minimum common node* in the ontology hierarchy. In our case this is *Construction*; then this is the object in **SchemaC**. Likewise, it is possible to compare each attribute from both classes. The additional information from Context and Metadata will help us for determining what is the semantic of each object in the process of assessing. A hierarchical structure is necessary for the attribute types and for the geometry types, Fig. 5.

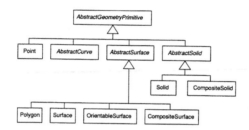

Fig. 5. Type Hierarchy of geometry types OpenGIS

4   Future Work and Conclusions

In this paper we have presented a framework for the integration of spatial data, spatial databases and most spatial sources. The ontology created from WordNet and SDTS lends its quality to the knowledge base. This work takes advantage of past approaches and tackles the particular domain of GIS integration. Also the matching process is associated to a federated architecture profiting from a more solid structure for the integration problem. One challenge will be the development of a complete production software for the integration of geographic information. But in contrast with other solutions, this is from the highest level of abstraction to the application level. For the continuation of this work, we are expecting the results from the W3C to adopt OWL for representing the ontologies and the new version of UMT for transforming XMI into some GML v3. The study with topology features and with the most complex structures and types in geographic data are in progress. On the other hand, the time dimension is out of the scope of this paper. Thereby, as a future work, it is necessary to take the temporal dimension into account.

Acknowledgments

Part of this work has been supported by: Ibero-Americana Spanish Agency of Cooperation (Spanish acronym AECI) MUTIS Program; and the Spanish Research Program PRONTIC under projects TIC2000-1723-C02-01. Special acknowledgment to M.Andrea Rodríguez (Department of Information Engineering and Computer Science, University of Ceoncepción, Chile) for her valuable contribution for this paper.

References

1. A. Abelló, M. Oliva, M. E. Rodríguez, and F. Saltor. The syntax of bloom99 schemas. Technical Report LSI-99-34-R, LSI-UPC, 1999.
2. V.R. Benjamins and D. Fensel. The ontological engineering initiative $(ka)^2$. In Nicola Guarino, editor, *Formal Ontology in Information Systems*, pages 287–301. IOS Press, 1998.
3. B. Bergamaschi, S. Castano, S. De Capitani di Vermercati, S. Montanari, and M. Vicini. An intelligent approach to information integration. In N Guarino, editor, *First International Conference on Formal Ontology in Information Systems*, pages 253–268, Terento, Italy, 1998.
4. Y. Bishr. *Semantic Aspects of Interoperable GIS*. PhD thesis, Wageningen Agricultural University, 1997.
5. Karla A.V. Borges, Clodoveu A. Davis, and Alberto H.F. Laender. Omt-g: An object-oriented data model for geographic applications. *GeoInformatica*, 5(3):221–260, Sep 2001.
6. W. Borst, J. Akkermans, and J. Top. Engineering ontologies. *International Journal of Human-Computers Studies. Special Issue on Using Explicit Ontologies in KBS Development*, (46):365–406, 1997.
7. M. Bright, A. Hurson, and S. Pakzad. Automated resolution of semantic heterogeneity in multidatabases. *ACM Transactions on Database Systems (TODS)*, 19(2):212–253, 1994.
8. Malú Castellanos, Fèlix Saltor, and Manuel García-Solaco. A canonical model for interoperability among object-oriented and relational databases. In *Distributed Object Management: Papers from the International Workshop on Distributed Management (IWDOM)*, pages 309–314. Morgan Kaufmann, Aug 1992.
9. C. Fellbaum, editor. *WordNet: An Electronic Lexical Database*. MIT Press, 1998.
10. FGDC. Geospatial standars. Retrieved from http://www.fgdc.gov/publications, 2002.
11. F. Fonseca, M. Egenhofer, P. Agouris, and C. Câmara. Using ontologies for integrated geographic information systems. *Transactions in GIS*, 6(3), Jun 2002.
12. Frederico Torres Fonseca. *Ontology-Driven Geographic Information*. PhD thesis, University of Maine, Orono, Maine 04469, May 2001.
13. S. Hayes and S. Ram. Multi-user view integration system (muvis). In *Proceedings of the 6th International Conference on Data Engineering*, Feb 1990.
14. Jeff Heflin and James Hendler. Semantic interoperability on the web. Extreme Markup Languages 2000, 2000. Retrieved from http://www.cs.umd.edu/projects/plus/SHOE/pubs/extreme2000.pdf.
15. V. Kashyap and A. Sheth. Semantic heterogeneity in global information systems: The role of metadata, context, and ontologies. In M Papazoglou and G Schlageter, editors, *Cooperative Information Systems: Tends and Directions*, pages 139–178, London, UK, 1998.

16. Pekka Kilpeläinen and Heikki Mannila. Ordered and unordered tree inclusion. *SAIM J.COMPUT*, 1995.
17. D. Lenat and R. Guha. *Building Large Knowledge Based Systems: Representation and Inference in the Cyc Project*. Reading, Mass,Addison-Wesley, 1990.
18. J. Madhavan, P.A. Bernstein, and E. Rahm. Generic schema matching with cupid. In *Proceedings of 27th VLDB*, pages 49–58, Roma, Italy, Sep 2001. Morgan Kaufmann.
19. E. Mena, V. Kashyap, A. Illarramendi, and A. Sheth. Domain specific ontologies for semantic information brokering on the global information infrastructure. In Nicola Guarino, editor, *Formal Ontology in Information Systems*. IOS press, 1998.
20. E. Mena, V. Kashyap, and A. Sheth. Observer: An approach for query processing in global information systems based on interoperation across pre-existing ontologies. In *CoopIS'96*, pages 14–25, Brussel, Belgium, 1996. IEEE Computer Society Press.
21. G. Miller, R. Beckwith, C. Fellbaum, D. Gross, and K. Miller. Introduction to wordnet: An on-line lexical database. *International Journal of Lexicography*, 3(4):235–244, 1990.
22. Villie Morocho, Lluís Pérez-Vidal, and Fèlix Saltor. Ontologies: Solving semantic heterogeneity in federated spatial database system. In *Proceedings of 5th International Conference on Enterprise Information System*, Angers, France, Apr 2003.
23. Jon Oldevik. Uml model transformation tool. Retrieved from http://www.modelbased.net/umt/, Sep 2002.
24. Object Management Group OMG. Omt unified modeling language specification v1.4. Retrieved from http://www.omg.org/, Sep 2001.
25. Object Management Group OMG. Xml metadata interchange (xmi) specification. Retrieved from http://www.omg.org/, Jan 2002.
26. OpenGIS. The opengis abstract specification. topic 0: Abstract specification overview. Retrieved May 2001, from http://www.opengis.org/techno/abstract/99-100r1.pdf, 1999.
27. Erhard Rahm and Philip A. Bernstein. A survey of approaches to automatic schema matching. *The VLDB Journal*, 10(4):334–350, 2001.
28. María Andrea Rodríguez. *Assessing Semantic Similarity Among Spatial Entity Classes*. PhD thesis, University of Maine, Orono, Maine 04469, May 2000.
29. Sheth and Larson. Federated database systems for managing distributed heterogeneous and autonomous databases. *ACM Computing Surveys*, 22(3), 1990.
30. A. Sheth, J. Larson, A. Cornellio, and S. Navathe. A tool for integrating conceptual schemas and user views. In *Proceedings of 4th International Conference on Data Engineering*, pages 176–183, 1988.
31. Amit P. Sheth. *Interoperating Geographic Information System*, chapter Changing focus on Interoperability from System, Syntax, Structure to Semantics, pages 5–29. Kluwer Academic Publisher, 1999.
32. Stefano Spaccapietra, Christine Parent, and Christelle Vangenot. Gis databases: From multiscale to multirepresentation. In *Proceedings of SARA 2000*, volume 1864 of *Lecture Notes in Computer Science*, pages 57–70, Horseshoe Bay, Texas, USA, Jul 2000. Springer.
33. Ph. Thiran, Abdelmajid Chougrani, Jean-Luc Hainaut, and Jean-Marc Hick. Case support for the development of federated information systems. In *Proceedings of the 3rd Workshop EFIS 2000*, pages 106–113, Dublin, Ireland, Jun 2000. EFIS, IOS Press.
34. USGS. View of the spatial data transfer standard (sdts). Retrieved May 2001, from http://mcmcweb.er.usgs.gov/sdts/standard.html, 1998.
35. W3C. Owl, web ontology language 1.0 reference(draft). Retrieved from http://www.w3.org/TR/2002/WD-owl-ref-20020729/, Jul 2002.
36. X3C. Xsl transformations (xslt). Retrieved from http://www.w3.org/TR/xslt, Nov 1999.
37. P. Zweigenbaum, B. Bachimont, J. Bouaud, J. Charlet, and J.F. Boisvieux. Issues in the structuring and acquisition of an ontology for medical language understanding. *Methods of Information in Medicine*, 34(1/2):15–24, 1995.

Structuring and Combining domain-specific Standards for Interoperability in Health Care

Susanne Pedersen and Wilhelm Hasselbring

University of Oldenburg, Software Engineering Group, Germany,
{susanne.pedersen|hasselbring}@informatik.uni-oldenburg.de,
WWW home page: http://se.informatik.uni-oldenburg.de

Abstract. Cooperation of health care providers is required to enable shared care. By means of efficient and effective communication, costs for health care shall be lowered and, at the same time, the quality of care shall increase. Well-known problems for interoperability with respect to correct communication among heterogeneous software systems of dissimilar health care providers emerge. A large amount of patient data has to be exchanged among the health care institutions to enable efficient shared care. In the past, various application systems for the different sectors in health care have been developed and deployed independently. To achieve effective communication, not only technical interfaces are required, but also common semantics for exchanged data. This paper focuses on problems of interoperability on the level of the application architecture, viz. Enterprise Application Integration [1]. Various health care standards are analysed, uniformly structured and put into a software architecture that enables interoperability based on domain-specific standards.

After a short overview of some relevant standards for communication and documentation in healthcare, we introduce our mediator-based architecture, which supports a top-down integration starting with standard-based integrated schemas [5,6]. The proposed architecture is evaluated in the context of the Epidemiological Cancer Registry Lower Saxony.

1 Standards for Interoperability in Health Care

The IEEE defines interoperability as the ability of two or more systems or components to exchange information and to use the information that has been exchanged [2,3]. Connecting heterogeneous information sources in health care usually implies problems of semantic interoperability [3]. Concerns of technical interoperability are not discussed in this paper.

A typical problem of semantic interoperability is that the same terms are often used for different concepts (homonyms) and that the same concepts are denoted by different terms (synonyms). Many standardization efforts aim at solving these problems [4]. Standards play an important role for ensuring a common understanding of transferred data among heterogeneous application systems [5]. Top-down integration, based on domain-specific standards, can result in scalable and flexible software architectures for federated information systems [6]. In the domain of health care there exist various standards for communication and documentation, which are introduced below. Later we will integrate these standards into a common metamodel.

1.1 Communication Standards

HL-7 (Health Level Seven) is a standard, which is used mainly for communication within hospitals [8, 9]. An accepted standard for exchanging digital images is DICOM (Digital Imaging and Communications in Medicine) [10]. Communication among general practitioners in Germany is supported by the BDT (Behandlungsdatenträger) standard [7]. We modelled the relationships among these standards by means of the standardized modeling language UML (Unified Modeling Language) [17]. Figure 1 illustrates the resulting structure of communication standards in health care as UML class diagram. The syntax of message structures defines multiple levels of partitions (hierarchical composition). This UML model defines a nomenclature resp. ontology for communication standards.

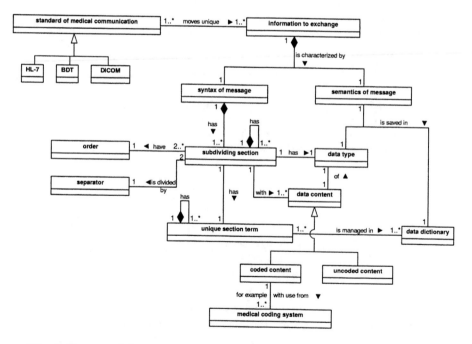

Fig. 1. Extract of the metamodel for communication standards in health care.

1.2 Documentation Standards

For medical documentation it is important to have standardized structures for documents and standardized coding systems for fields in the documents (terminologies, taxonomies, ontologies, nomenclatures, etc.).

Electronic Healthcare Records

It can be expected that electronic healthcare records (EHCR), based on medical terminology, will be at the center of future health care information systems. Important standardisation projects in this field are EHCR of CEN (Comit Europen de Normalisation) and the CDA (Clinical Document Architecture) of the HL-7 Group [9, 11]. The three different levels of CDA for example offer a way to incrementally add (semantical) markup, based on the HL-7 RIM (Reference Information Model). Currently, only CDA Level One has been defined, CDA Level Two is under work.

The goal of the SCIPHOX project (Standardisation of Communication between Information Systems in Physician Offices and Hospitals using XML) is to define a standardised report (e.g. referral, discharge letter) based on the standards CDA and XML to exchange reports between BDT and HL-7 domain [18]. SCIPHOX defines six semantical units to describe and structure diagnoses, therapies etc. to a greater detail than CDA Level One. The results of SCIPHOX will influence the definition of CDA Level Two.

Again, we modelled the relationships among the relevant documentation standards in the UML to later combine them on a metalevel with the communication standards. Figure 2 displays our nomenclature for documentation standards.

Medical Coding Systems

Medical coding systems are used within documents to code measurements, diagnoses etc. They standardize terminology. Examples are the ICD (International Statistical Classification of Diseases and Related Health Problems) and SNOMED (Systematized Nomenclature of Human and Veterinary Medicine). In [4] we introduce a nomenclature of coding systems, which specifies in the UML the connections among several relevant medical coding systems. Figure 3 displays an extract. At the heart of this model, you can see the semiotic triad. On a meta level, we combine this nomenclature with the standards of communication in Section 1.3.

1.3 Combining the Healthcare Standards

Metadata is important for federated information systems to achieve flexibility for evolution and means for overcoming heterogeneity [14]. Figure 4 displays the relationships among the communication and documentation standards that were introduced in the previous subsections. For example the nomenclature for communication standards contains metadata for the relevant communication standards HL-7, BDT and DICOM. Standards for documentation such as electronic

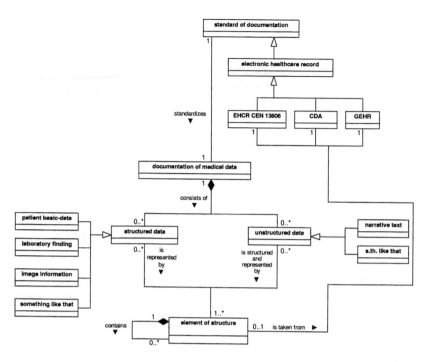

Fig. 2. Extract of the metamodel for documentation standards in health care.

healthcare records use medical coding systems. CDA, the electronic healthcare record defined by the HL-7 group, is formulated in HL-7.

2 Mediator-based Software Architecture

Our goal is to develop a flexible and scalable software architecture, which enables interoperability among the various institutions providing health care. This architecture uses the meta models for health care standards which were introduced in Section 1. Figure 5 illustrates our mediator-based architecture, which follows the mediator metaphor [12, 13] with facilitators and component mediators.

The mediation layer, which enables interoperability based on domain-specific standards, consists of wrappers, component mediators, facilitators, optional application mediators and various metadata stores. For each domain-specific standard for documentation there exits a component mediator, for example the CDA component mediator. The documentation component mediator uses the metadata from the nomenclature for documentation standards (Section 1.2). This model illustrates the correspondences (mappings) among the specific component mediators. Metadata from the nomenclature for coding systems helps to mediate among the different medical coding systems, which are used in medical documentation. Several facilitators manage the specific domain models, for example an HL-7 facilitator for the HL-7 reference information model (RIM).

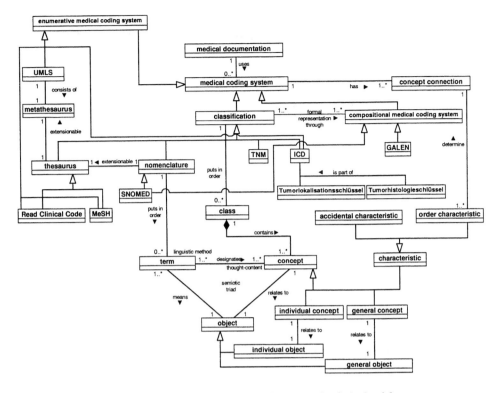

Fig. 3. Extract of the metamodel for coding standards in health care.

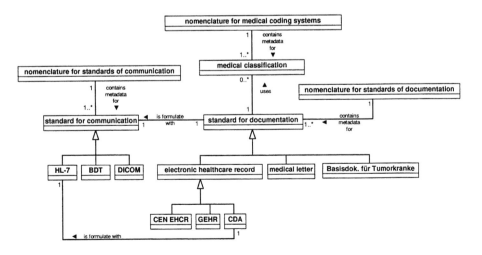

Fig. 4. Relationships among the communication and documentation standards.

A communication facilitator coordinates as facilitator by means of a nomenclature for communication standards. This way, we support a top-down integration starting with the domain-specific standards [5, 6]. Complete mappings are not always possible. When application structures and standard structures harmonize the quality of the mappings increases. This also means that an evolution of standards themselves is useful and required.

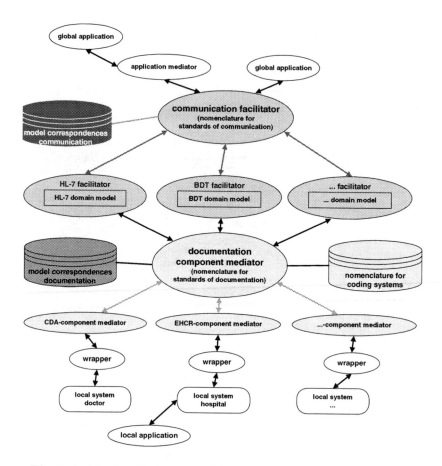

Fig. 5. Architecture for interoperability among institutions in health care.

3   Case Study

Our approach to structuring communication and documentation standards in health care for managing interoperability in federated information systems is currently under practical evaluation, whereby the Epidemiological Cancer Registry Lower Saxony (EKN) [15] serves as a case study. With the procedure suggested in [16], we selected for this case study HL-7 and BDT as standards for communication, and ICD-O (International Statistical Classification of Diseases and Related Health Problems - Oncology) as the coding standard. The "Basisdokumentation für Tumorkranke" (base documentation for tumour diseases) from the "Deutsche Krebsgesellschaft e.V." (German cancer association) and the "Arbeitsgemeinschaft Deutscher Tumorzentren" (working group of German tumour centres) was selected as the appropriate documentation standard as a basis for an integrated model. The heterogeneous documents corresponding to the epidemiological cancer registries from the different reporter groups are integrated in a top-down manner starting with the selected domain-specific standards.

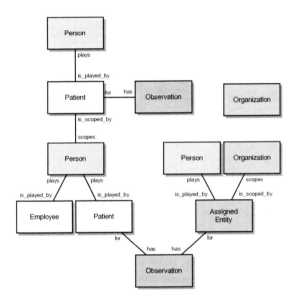

Fig. 6. Corresponding classes of the HL-7 RIM to the EKN from [19].

Figure 6 shows those classes derived from the HL-7 RIM, which correspond to the structure of the EKN. The generic HL-7 RIM has a high degree of abstraction and therefore varied possibilities for its mapping to the base documentation for tumour diseases [19]. On the other hand it was not possible in this case study to get a complete mapping from HL-7 RIM to the base documentation. Some relations, e.g. information from death certificates could not be modeled in HL-7 RIM. So there is a need for evolution of standards in health care [5]. As mapping language an extended version of BRIITY (Bridging Heterogeneity) [20] was used.

Figure 7 illustrates the instantiation of our more general architecture in Figure 5 to the specific requirements of the EKN. The mappings among the heterogeneous data models are coordinated by a control component.

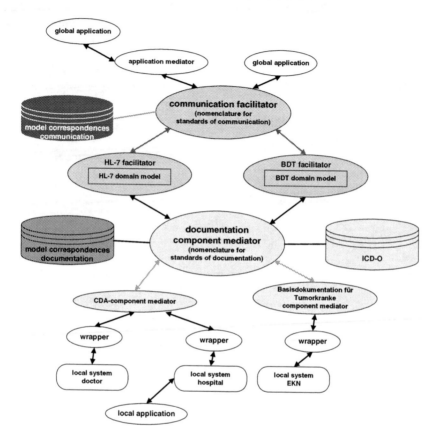

Fig. 7. Architecture of our EKN case study.

4 Summary

Domain-specific standards play an important role for achieving semantic interoperability among federated information systems. Both, standards for communication formats and standards for documents with an appropriate standardized coding system (nomenclature) are required for a holistic solution.

In the present paper, we presented our efforts for uniform structuring of these relevant standards. The proposed mediator-based architecture offers a flexible and scalable approach for sustainable evolution. This approach is based on a separation of concerns for managing the global, integrated models and the individual mappings from local component models into the integrated domain-specific models. This way scalability is enabled. The proposed architecture is evaluated within the context of an epidimiologic cancer registry system. Our goal is to develop a flexible and scalable software architecture, which enables interoperability among the various institutions in health care. This architecture is based on the presented meta models for health care standards. Because of our uniform specification of relevant standards for communication and documentation by means of the standardised UML, appropriate metadata for a transformation among heterogeneous models is provided for achieving interoperability among federated information systems of the various institutions in health care.

There is a need for evolution of standards themselves. Current standards often do not fit properly to application areas, which not in the medical main stream, such as epidemiological cancer registries.

References

1. Hasselbring, W.: Information System Integration. Communications of the ACM. **43** (2000) 33–38
2. Institute of Electrical and Electronics Engineers (IEEE): URL: http://www.ieee.org. Retrieved: 31.08.2002.
3. Ingenerf, J., Reiner, J., Seik, B.: Standardized terminological services enabling semantic interoperabiliy between distributed and heterogeneous systems. International Journal of Medical Informatics. **64** (2001) 223–240
4. Pedersen, S., Hasselbring, W.: Begriffssysteme für die medizinische Dokumentation (nomenclatura for medical documentation). Tagungsband der 7. Fachtagung des Deutschen Verbandes Medizinischer Dokumentare e.V. (2002) 47–52
5. Hasselbring, W.: The Role of Standards for Interoperating Information Systems. Jakobs, K. (Publisher): Information Technology Standards and Standardization: A Global Perspective. Idea Group Publishing, Hershey, PA (2000) 116–130
6. Hasselbring, W.: Web Data Integration for E-Commerce Applications. IEEE MultiMedia. **9(1)** (2002) 16–25
7. Zentralinstitut für die kassenärztliche Versorgung in der Bundesrepublik Deutschland: URL: http://zi-koeln.de. Retrieved: 02.04.2002.
8. Heitmann, K., Blobel, B., Dudeck, J.: HL-7 Kommunikationsstandard in der Medizin: Kurzeinführung und Information. Verlag Alexander Mönch. 1. Auflage (1999)
9. Health Level Seven: URL: http://www.hl7.org. Retrieved: 07.03.2002.
10. Digital Imaging and Communications in Medicine: URL: http://medical.nema.org/dicom.html. Retrieved: 14.05.2002.
11. CEN/TC251: URL: http://www.centc251.org. Retrieved: 06.06.2002.
12. Wiederhold, G.: Mediators in the Architecture of Future Information Systems. IEEE Computers. **25 No.3** (1992) 38–49
13. Wiederhold, G.: Mediation in Information Systems. ACM Computing Surveys. **27 No.2** (1995) 265–267
14. Busse, S., Kutsche, R.-D., Leser, U., Weber, H.: Federated Information Systems: Concepts, Terminology and Architectures. Forschungsberichte des Fachbereichs Informatik 99-9. Technische Universität Berlin. (1999)

15. Rohde, M., Wietek, F.: Das Datenschema für das Epidemiologische Krebsregister Niedersachsen. 4. überarbeitete Auflage, OFFIS, Oldenburg, 1999. URL: http://www.krebsregister-niedersachsen.de.
16. Lagendijk, P., Stegwee, R.: Healthcare Information and Communication Standards Framework. Stegwee, R., Spill, T. (editor) Strategies for Healthcare Information Systems. (2001) 66–77
17. Oestereich, B.: Objektorientierte Softwareentwicklung: Analyse und Design mit der Unified Modeling Language. R. Oldenbourg Verlag. 4. aktualisierte Auflage (1999)
18. SCIPHOX: URL: http://www.sciphox.de. Retrieved: 05.12.2001.
19. Willms, W.: Eine Abbildung des HL7 Referenzinformationsmodells auf die Datenstruktur im Epidemiologischen Krebsregister Niedersachsen. Diplomarbeit Fachbereich Informatik, Universität Oldenburg. (2002)
20. Sauter, G.: Interoperabilität von Datenbanksystemen bei struktureller Heterogenität. Band 47. Infix-Verlag, St. Augustin. 1998

Four-level Architecture for Closure in Interoperability

Nick Rossiter[1] and Michael Heather[2]

[1] School of Informatics, Northumbria University, NE1 8ST, UK,
nick.rossiter@unn.ac.uk,
WWW home page: http://computing.unn.ac.uk/staff/CGNR1/
[2] Sutherland Building, Northumbria University, NE1 8ST, UK

Abstract. A definition of types in an information system is given from real-world abstractions through data constructs, schema and definitions to physical data values. Category theory suggests that four levels are sufficient to provide ultimate closure for computational types to construct information systems. The Godement calculus provides rules governing the composition of the mappings at different levels. Examples of information systems are reviewed in terms of the four-level architecture including IRDS, the Grid, the semantic web and MOF/MDA.

1 The four fundamental levels and their formalisation

Interoperability is still a major problem in information systems. Most achievements have been with systems using a similar model or paradigm. Where heterogeneous systems are involved, progress has required much manual adjustment to mappings. Recently the development of the Grid has exposed the great difficulty of employing data held in formal database systems as opposed to operating system files [Watson, 2002]. Using higher-order logic we build on existing work [Rossiter, Nelson and Heather, 2001] to review some examples and their reliability for applications of interoperability and cross-platform software.

The whole subject of relating different systems emerges in federated information systems (FIS) as the core issue. The term *level* is used in FIS in a subtly different way [Conrad *et al*, 1997] to that employed in this paper so we start with a brief description of our architecture. One instance of the fundamental levels in Fig 1 is a representation of a single platform, paradigm or model. Level 1 would be real-world type abstractions, level 2 the type constructs available, level 3 the data types and level 4 the named values.

Constructive mathematics attempts to develop logically what can work in practice and can therefore provide the necessary universal typing for interoperability of heterogeneous data systems with consistency and quality assurance in the real-world. Category theory [Barr and Wells, 1990] is particularly appropriate for modelling multi-level relationships for it is essentially concerned with links between objects. In categorial terms each of the four levels is defined as a category (i.e. a type) as shown in Fig 2. Between each level there is a higher-order function, a functor, which ensures that certain consistency requirements are met in the mapping between the source and target categories. The four levels from the top are defined as the categories **CONCEPTS** (abstractions), **CONSTRUCTS**, **SCHEMA** and **DATA** with the mappings between them as shown in the diagram.

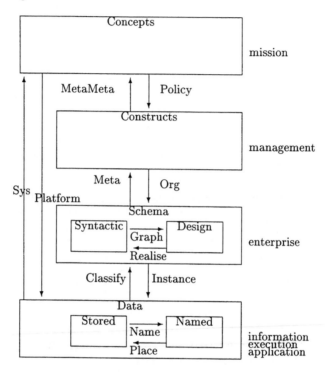

Fig. 1. Interpretation of Fundamental Levels informally

Adjointness [Barr and Wells, 1990] characterises the unique relationship between a lower-limit functor (F) that preserves co-limits and an upper-limit functor (G) which preserves limits, written $F \dashv G$, that is G is right-adjoint to F. The multi-level application shown in Fig 2 involves the composition of adjoints, that is an expression is derived in which two or more adjoints are adjacent to each other. It is part of the power of category theory that adjoints can be composed in the same way as other arrows. For example consider the adjoints shown in Fig 3 where **CC** is the category **CONCEPTS**, **CS CONSTRUCTS**, **SM SCHEMA** and **DT DATA**.

Then we may have six adjoints (if the conditions are satisfied):
$$I \dashv C; \qquad O \dashv M; \qquad P \dashv A; \qquad I \circ O \dashv M \circ C; \qquad O \circ P \dashv A \circ M;$$
$$I \circ O \circ P \dashv A \circ M \circ C$$
where P is the functor *Policy*, O *Org*, I *Instance*, A *MetaMeta*, M *Meta* and C *Classify*. We can construct the 4-tuple to represent the composed adjunctions defined in Fig 2: $< IOP, AMC, AM\bar{\bar{\eta}}_{cc}OP \bullet A\bar{\eta}_{cc}P \bullet \eta_{cc}, \bar{\bar{\epsilon}}_{dt} \bullet I\bar{\epsilon}_{dt}C \bullet IO\epsilon_{dt}MC >$.

If the conditions of this adjunction are met, we can represent the composed adjunction *Platform* $\dashv$ *Sys* by the 4-tuple $< Platform, Sys, \eta_{cc}, \epsilon_{dt} >$: **CC** $\longrightarrow$

84

DT where $Platform = IOP$, $Sys = AMC$, η_{cc} is the unit of adjunction, ϵ_{dt} is the counit of adjunction, cc is an object in **CC** and dt an object in **DT**.

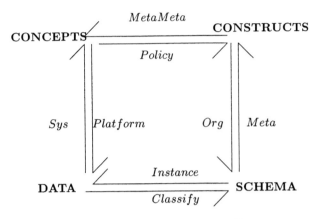

Fig. 2. Four Levels in Functorial Terms

This adjunction can be evaluated for each application giving a collection of 4-tuples. Comparison of these 4-tuples then gives the mechanism for computational type closure. The ability to compose adjoints naturally means that we can combine well together such diverse features as policy, organization and data in a single arrow.

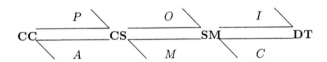

Fig. 3. Composition of Adjoints

The overall composition gives a simple representation for conceptual purposes; the individual mappings enable the transformations to be followed in detail at each stage and provide a route for implementation.

2 Comparing one System with Another

Adjunctions give the relationships between one level and another. We can also approach the problem by considering a direct mapping between one instance of the four-level architecture and another as in Fig 4. Here for simplicity the mappings are viewed in one direction only. Two systems are compared, one involving categories **CC**, **CS**, **SM** and **DT**, the other **CC**, **CS'**, **SM'** and **DT'**. **CC** is the same in both systems as there is one universal type for concepts. As in Fig 3, the functors relate the categories. We have now though added natural transformations to relate the mapping between one functor and another.

85

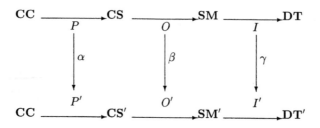

Fig. 4. Comparison of Mappings in two Systems

If we follow the constructive principles of category theory, then the composition of these arrows is natural. The Godement calculus ([Godement, 1958]; [Barr and Wells, 1990], pp 94-97) gives a number of rules governing the compositions. Rules G2 and G3 say that the composition of functors and natural transformations is associative so that for instance:

$$(I'O')\alpha = I'(O'\alpha); \quad \gamma(OP) = (\gamma O)P$$

Rule G3 says that natural transformations may be composed with each other:

$$\gamma\beta = (\gamma O) \circ (I'\beta); \quad \beta\alpha = (\beta P) \circ (O'\alpha)$$

The consequence of this for interoperability is that a categorical approach ensures that the various arrows of different types can be composed with each other, irrespective of their level in the system. Equations can be derived, representing an equality of paths, with unknown components that can be determined from an evaluation of the known properties. For instance with the path IOP from **CC** $\longrightarrow$ **CS** $\longrightarrow$ **SM** $\longrightarrow$ **DT** defining an object-oriented system, then the path $I'O'\alpha$ from **CC** $\longrightarrow$ **CS'** $\longrightarrow$ **SM'** $\longrightarrow$ **DT'** would define a relational representation if P' maps onto relational constructs in the category **CS'**.

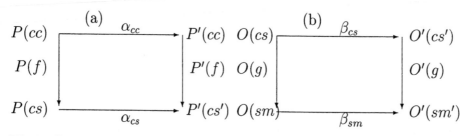

Fig. 5. Commuting Target Square for Natural Transformations: (a) $\alpha : P \longrightarrow P'$, comparing policies; (b) $\beta : O \longrightarrow O'$, comparing use of constructs

In category theory four levels are required to define an arrow as unique up to natural isomorphism. The four levels are: 1) object or identity arrow (within a category), 2) category (comparing objects), 3) functor (comparing categories) and 4) natural transformation (comparing functors). No more levels are required. An arrow comparing natural transformations is a natural transformation. Two squares, derived from Fig 4, are shown above. Fig 5(a) must commute for each arrow $f : cc \longrightarrow cs$ if α is to be a natural transformation. Similarly Fig 5(b) must commute for each arrow $g : cs \longrightarrow sm$ if β is to be a natural transformation. Viewed in this way a natural transformation is not a layer above functors and functions. The levels are interwoven with natural transformations considering how every arrow defined at the lowest level is mapped.

If we write the arrow: $\delta : \alpha \longrightarrow \beta$ then δ is a composition $\beta \circ \alpha$. An arrow from one natural transformation to another gives a composition of the natural transformations, not a new level ([Barr and Wells, 1990], at p.85). The four levels of concepts, constructs, schema and data are viewed in Fig 2 as four categories connected by a composition of three functors. An alternative view, shown in Fig 6, is closer to the four levels inherent in category theory. The fundamental levels are considered to be data values, named values, classified values and contrasted representation corresponding in category theory to object, category, functor and natural transformation respectively. The natural transformations are now the duals of those shown earlier in Fig 4 as indicated by the * superscript.

alternative funda-mental levels	category theory levels	four levels of Fig 4
1. data values	objects (identity arrows)	id_{dt}
2. named values	category	**DT**
3. classified values	functor	C : **DT** $\longrightarrow$ **SM**
4. contrasted representation	natural transformation	$\alpha^* \circ \beta^*$

Fig. 6. Alternative Interpretation of Levels in the Architecture

This view does not supersede the earlier one which is more useful for system design with its similarity to the ANSI/SPARC three-level architecture. The alternative view though may have some potential for interoperability where comparisons are an inherent part of the methodology with natural transformations as ultimate closure. It can be seen that the addition of further levels is possible but nothing is gained by it type-wise. Thus addition of an extra level to the top of Fig 1 simply results in the top level being a composition of three arrows rather than two. The practical consequence is that a fifth level is equivalent to an alternative fourth level. The meta-meta level gives ultimate closure of types.

3 Levels in applications

Four existing approaches to interoperability were examined to see how they compare in giving a genuine four-level strategy for tackling the problem of interoperability [Rossiter, Nelson and Heather, 2003]:

1. Information Resource Dictionary System [Gradwell, 1990]
2. Grid Construction [Watson, 2002]
3. Data Exchange Languages [Berners-Lee *et al*, 2001]
4. Metaobjects in the Model-driven Architecture [Bezivin, 2001]

The Information Resource Dictionary Standard (IRDS) did provide four levels but ANSI downgraded this standard and its influence has been less than anticipated. More recently ISO has begun again to value a four-level architecture with the consideration of a meta-meta *model* in work on comparing models. Systems developed recently, claiming to provide interoperability, such as MOF are able to provide considerable assistance within a paradigm but appear to lack the top level, mapping abstractions to constructions, necessary to achieve interoperability across paradigms. Moreover, recent work has suggested that future effort with MOF [Habela, Roantree and Subieta, 2002] should flatten the metamodel to reduce complexity and to support extendibility. Both IRDS and MOF are data-driven approaches in a general sense. The semantic web takes a different approach, being partially data-driven through RDF but also relying on agent-based technology for resolving mismatches. The semantic web therefore appears to lack the two top levels of concepts and constructs but the use of ontologies and agents may compensate to some extent at least for some of this loss. The Grid also lacks the top two levels for data addressing and its potential will not be realised until this deficiency is tackled.

To conclude the generality of current techniques for interoperability is in doubt. The definition of the four levels necessary for providing interoperability, the availability of the Godement calculus for composing mappings formed at different levels and the specifications of the adjointness between the levels and of pullback categories representing relationships, all add coherence through a categorical approach to interoperability.

References

[Barr and Wells, 1990] Barr, M, & Wells, C, *Category Theory for Computing Science.*
[Berners-Lee *et al*, 2001] Berners-Lee, T, Hendler, J, & Lassila, O, The Semantic Web, *Scientific American*, May 2001.
[Bezivin, 2001] Bezivin, J, From Object Composition to Model Transformation with the MDA, *3rd ICEIS*, Setubal, invited paper.
[Conrad *et al*, 1997] Conrad, S, Eaglestone, B, Hasselbring, W, Roantree, M, Saltor, F, Schnhoff, M, Strssler, M, & Vermeer, M W W, Research Issues in Federated Database Systems: Report EFDBS '97 Workshop, *SIGMOD Rec* **26**(4) 54-56.
[Godement, 1958] Godement, R, *Théorie des faisceaux*, Hermann.
[Gradwell, 1990] Gradwell, D J L, The Arrival of IRDS Standards, *8th BNCOD*, York 1990, Pitman 196-209.
[Habela, Roantree and Subieta, 2002] Habela, P, Roantree, M, & Subieta, K, Flattening the Metamodel for Object Databases, *ADBIS 2002*, 263-276.
[Rossiter, Nelson and Heather, 2001] Rossiter, B N, Nelson, D A, & Heather, M A, A Universal Technique for Relating Heterogeneous Data Models, *3rd ICEIS*, Setbal, I 96-103.
[Rossiter, Nelson and Heather, 2003] Rossiter, N, Nelson, D A, & Heather, M A, Formalizing Types with Ultimate Closure for Middleware Tools in Information Systems Engineering, 5th ICEIS, Angers, France 23-26 April 8pp.
[Watson, 2002] Watson, P, *Databases and the Grid*, Computing Science Tech Rep no.755, University of Newcastle upon Tyne 16pp.

Designing a Metadata-based Infrastructure for E-Learning

Wolfgang Sigel[1], Susanne Busse[1], Ralf-Detlef Kutsche[1], and Meike Klettke[2]

[1] Technische Universität Berlin {wsigel, sbusse, rkutsche}@cs.tu-berlin.de
[2] Universität Rostock meike@informatik.uni-rostock.de

Abstract. Today lifelong learning becomes a major issue in order to fulfill the requirements imposed in business, education, etc. Also it has been realized that the expenses for continous training on the job are quite high. Thus there has to be a trade-off between the need for training and the expenditure necessary for such efforts. In the E-Learning community attempts are being made to find solutions for this quest. Currently in the 'New Economy Project' [3] efforts are being undertaken to build didactic material for the economic, communication and information sciences. In the MEFIS project one of the main aspects is to research the usage of metadata within federated information systems (FIS). This article shows how metadata can support the construction, usage and evolution of systems for advanced vocational training. It is also shown that FIS represent an appropriate architectural infrastructure for this kind of training.

1 Introduction

This article exhibits research activities currently being undertaken within the MEFIS-project [4] - a joint cooperation between Technische Universität Berlin and Universität Rostock. A lot of applications require the integration of various information sources. These sources usually start out their existence as a response to the needs of local users and therefore the diversity being covered by these sources in terms of hard- and software plattforms, DBMS's, data models, query languages, etc is rather vast. The necessity of maintaining the local day-to-day operations renders the seamless integration of these sources a difficult task. Federated architectures aim to provide a solution to this kind of problem. A lot of research has been done in this area but still the building and maintaining of a federation is far from being a trivial task. A key aspect within the MEFIS - project is to examine the enhancements which can be achieved through a metadata-based approach and to specify facilities and methodologies in support of such a metadata-oriented strategy. In this article we start out by motivating our metadata-based approach with a scenario related to the domain of e-learning (section 2). Next, the notion of metadata (section 3) is introduced, focusing particularly on the outcome of the standardisation effort being undertaken by

---

[3] project homepage is http://www.dialekt.cedis.fu-berlin.de/neweconomy

[4] project homepage is http://cis.cs.tu-berlin.de/Forschung/Projekte/mevolfis

the 'Learning Technology Standards Committee' (LTSC), since its fruition - published as the 'Learning Object Metadata' (LOM) - is being used in our project. Subsequently, we illustrate how federated information systems (FIS - section 4) provide a perfect architectural environment for this kind of scenario. The usage of metadata in order to perform queries (section 5) and to evolve federated information systems (section 6) is presented before we conclude and give an outlook on future work (section 7).

2 An Application Scenario: Workflow-Embedded Training

A company's IT department introduces relational database technologogy. As a consequence, the database administrator and programmer, Peter D., 53, has to be trained in relational database design, administration, SQL programming, embedded SQL wrt. the programming languages commonly in use within the enterprise, and finally about specific features of the chosen database product. As it turns out, the latter is provided from the software company whose product has been purchased. Peter and his boss have found a provider for IT e-learning materials. However, the cost for this didactic material is quite high. In order to reduce the necessary expenditures Peter wants that his previously acquired knowledge in E/R modeling is taken into account. A successful selection of didactic materials also has to consider dependencies amongst the individual e-learning entities: some require that other subjects have been covered as a prerequisite. Taking into account Peter's overall intended learning goal and the dependency among the material this search yields seven modules (M1 ... M7). As each separate learning material requires a certain minimum learning time the total learning time necessary for these selected modules sums up to an amount of 38 hours. In this respect Peter's boss wants, that the time spent for further education does not exceed a total of 30 hours. The learning environment considers these constraints by querying the metadata as well as the content (or content portions), suggesting two similar solutions:

- both of them omit the module 'M5 - RDBMS Installation and Configuration' (covered by the special product features training),
- one decides to omit 'M2 - RDB Design' (since it is partially covered by Peter's knowledge in E/R modeling) and the other mandates 'M3 - RDB Design Optimization' (as a nice feature for the future),
- both of them omit one of the case studies in module 'M6 - Application Examples', thereby reducing the learning time for M6 by 50 per cent.

The modules "M1 - General Intro into RDBMS", "M4 - SQL and Embedded SQL" and "M7 - Maintenance and User Support" are kept in the individual course for Peter. Depending on the quality of Peter's knowledge on modeling and DB design, one could consider, whether M1 should be omitted in favour of M2. Finally, Peter has to decide on his prefered 'learning path' (whereby each path satisfies the temporal constraints):

- M1 $\longrightarrow$ M2 $\longrightarrow$ M4 $\longrightarrow$ M6.1 $\longrightarrow$ M7 (30 hours)
- M1 $\longrightarrow$ M3 $\longrightarrow$ M4 $\longrightarrow$ M6.1 $\longrightarrow$ M7 (29 hours)
- M2 $\longrightarrow$ M3 $\longrightarrow$ M4 $\longrightarrow$ M6.1 $\longrightarrow$ M7 (28 hours)

3 The Crucial Role of Metadata in E-Learning

At present, a lot of attention is directed towards the design, development and distribution of educational materials. Attempts are made to reuse elementary objects in different learning contexts and to use them to build more complex instructional components. These learning objects can be delivered over the Internet or other infrastructures and can also be accessed simultaneously by numerous people. In terms of advanced vocational training these learning objects play a crucial role and they can appear in different granularities - from atomic objects (e.g. tables, pictures, paragraphs of text) up to quite complex objects (e.g exams, experiments, self assessments). If a certain amount of these objects are semantically related - for example they contain a motivation and a solution to a specific problem - then we will call this unit a learning module. A complete course on a certain subject will be composed out of a set of these modules. All people are different and this applies also for learners. Therefore different learners wanting to cover a new subject usually have different amounts of previous knowledge and their ways of tapping the subject will also be quite different. As a consequence each learner will embark on a different strategy in completing his learning task. We will call the sequence of covered learning modules from the starting point to the goal of the learning task (where the learner has mastered the subject) - a learning path. Within the 'New Economy'- Project [12], the production of learning objects has been a major issue. In order to make the most effective use of this didactic material, it needs to be described in such a way that e.g. learners, course instructors, representatives for advanced vocational training can find the approriate material. A common shared vocabulary that is able to provide the above mentioned different user groups with the ability to identify relevant properties of learning objects and to describe those object properties in an appropriate granularity would be desirable. We believe that metadata can fulfill these kinds of requirements. In our project, we use the 'Standard for Learning Object Metadata' (LOM - specified in [9]) supplied by the 'Learning Technology Standardization Committee' (LTSC) of the IEEE as a reference vocabulary. In figure 1 we abstract from most of the details and demonstrate how the LOM-Base Scheme Entry 'Relation.Kind' helps us to express the constraint in terms of learning time from our scenario. We have a number of linked learning objects forming a directed graph whereby the labeled arcs indicate a dependency relation between learning objects. The label 'requires' corresponds to entries in the LOM-element 'Relation.Kind'. Within this figure we have two different learning sequences (indicated by dashed/solid line). In each one of them the overall time necessary to complete the initial learning goal is computed: 1 hour and 50 minutes (= 20 + 30 + 15 + 45 minutes) for the first and 55 minutes (= 20 + 25 + 10 minutes) for the second path.

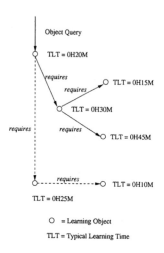

Object Query

TLT = 0H20M

requires

requires

TLT = 0H15M

TLT = 0H30M

requires

requires

TLT = 0H45M

requires

TLT = 0H10M

TLT = 0H25M

O = Learning Object

TLT = Typical Learning Time

Fig. 1. sample graph displaying dependencies among learning objects

4 Federated Information Systems Providing an Architectural Infrastructure for E-Learning

The following reasons indicate the usage of a metadata based mediator as an architecture for this kind of scenario: (1) we have more than one data source providing didactic materials (2) the data provided by the sources need not necessarily all be structured, semi-structured and unstructured data might occur as well (3)we do not want to force the user having to know about the information and structure of export schemas in order to maintain and create federation schemas (4) our scenario entails read-only access to the stored data (5) we think that the usage of metadata (see section 3) is a useful asset therefore our architecture should support that view. See ([5],[3],[19],[4]) for a classification of information systems, to see how our ideas fit into the scheme. As stated in our application scenario (see section 2) the user accesses the mediator in order to query for learning objects with certain properties. In section 3 we pointed out, that the LOM-standard is an appropriate means in terms of identifying crucial aspects of learning objects. Therefore our mediator schema has to support LOM-specific queries in order for a user to find appropriate objects. The global mediator schema is constructed out of the schemas located on the metainformation level. This is usually a non-trivial task (see the literature on schema integration, e.g. [17], [2], [21],[8]). The effort in building the global mediator schema can therefore be reduced substantially if the schemas on the metainformation level are congruent to each other, for example if they all follow the same standard like LOM. In this case the resulting global mediator schema would also be 'LOM - congruent'. For a query against the global mediator schema to be successful appropriate mappings between the mediator schema and the schemas on the level below - the metainformation level - have to be defined. In the case of 'LOM - congruent' schemas on the metainformation level those mappings are fairly simple since the schema elements on those two different levels can be correlated 1 to 1. In figure 2 we present a LOM - specific instantiation of our generic infrastructure. For many people the usage of the LOM - standard in its full

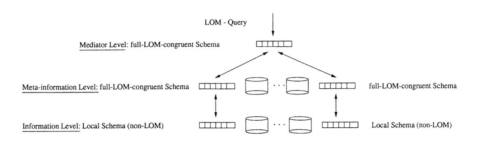

Fig. 2. mediator based on LOM - congruent metainformation

breadth might be a bit overwhelming. For example the 'New Economy Project' decided to use only a subset of the LOM - standard. So how would such a constellation - having 'full-LOM-congruent' and 'LOM-subset-congruent' schemas on the same metainformation level - effect the construction of the global mediator schema ? Figure 3 illustrates this situation. In fact the effort for constructing the global mediator schema would still be the same: we would still have a 'full-LOM-congruent' schema on the mediator level. Still the schema elements on mediator and metainformation level could be correlated 1 to 1, the only difference being that the mappings between a 'LOM-subset-congruent' schema and the mediator schema would be partial (there are some schema elements on the mediator schema for which no equivalent elements exist on the 'LOM-subset-congruent' schema).

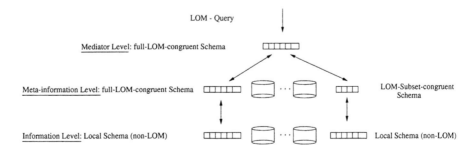

Fig. 3. mediator based on 'LOM' - and 'LOM-subset' - congruent metainformation

5 Query Processing in Federated Information Systems

In federated information systems different kinds of data and documents can be stored. We add metadata that describe the data sources more detailed. Different kinds of queries can be realised in a FIS. Thereby, we can distinguish the following criteria:

- the data being queried: either the data or documents itself and/or the metadata.
- the query-result: queries can deliver complete data or documents or fragments of these.

According to both criteria, we can distinguish the following four cases. All of these cases are relevant for our scenarios.

1. A user can query the metadata and receives the complete document as a result. Therefore, query-methods for metadata (e.g. database queries or XML queries according to the format of the metadata) are necessary. As a result a complete document (e.g. XML, HTML, PPT, Winword) is delivered. These kinds of queries are quite common and easy to implement, since it is not necessary to analyse the documents themselves, neither at the time of posing the query or when presenting the result: the documents are always treated as a whole. An example for these kinds of queries is the following one. We assume for the query that the metadata are organized in a relational database and use a SQL99 [13] query. Further, we assume that the documents are stored in the same database in the attribute content. In our sample query, we want to find all modules dealing with relational database design.

```
select general_title, content
from modules
where (general_keywords.contains('"relational database design"') =1)
and ((general_language='en') or (general_language='de'))
```

2. A user can query the data or documents and receive the complete document as a result. These kinds of queries are equivalent to committing a search in our e-learning scenario. It requires query-methods for data (information retrieval queries, XML queries or database queries depending on the format of the data or documents). The documents have to be analysed in order to e.g. make them accessible via indexing-mechanisms for information retrieval queries or XML queries. As a result, a complete document (e.g. XML, HTML, PPT, Winword) is delivered. At the time of presenting the result no document analysis is necessary. An example is the following one. Here the query exploits the documents itself. We use SQL/MM Full-Text [20] syntax for demonstration. In the sample query, we want to get all modules that contain information about oracle and configuration parameters.

```
select general_title, content
from modules
where content.contains (' ("oracle") near "configuration parameters"
       within 10 words any order ') =1
```

3. A user can query the metadata and receive a section of the document as a result. These queries afford query-methods for metadata (database queries, XML queries according to the format of the metadata). As a result one gets a section of a document, whereby the document needs to be analysed. In XML documents we can use XML query languages. The analysis of the documents and the result construction is not trivial if the documents are in other formats like HTML, PPT, or Winword. With SQL, we cannot deliver a part of a document as a result. Therefore, we give an example how such queries can be expressed with XQuery [1]. Here, the abstract of the module M6 shall be delivered as result.

```
for $x in //modules
where $x/module/@number= 'M6'
return $x/content/abstract
```

4. A user can query the data or documents and receive a section of the document as result. These queries are equivalent to a search within our e-learning scenario. Query methods for data (information retrieval queries, XML queries or database queries depending on the data or document format are necessary for searching in the documents directly. As a result the user gets a section of the data or the document. The document has to be analysed for result construction. For XML documents we can apply XML query languages. In cases like HTML, PPT, and Winword the analysis and result creation are difficult to perform. This scenario is typical for exploitation of data in relational or object oriented databases. The following XQuery delivers from a list of examples in module M6 the one with the theme customer data management.

```
for $x in //modules
where $x/module/@number= 'M6'
  for $y in $x/content
  where $y/example/@thema='customer data management'
  return <application_example>
          <title>customer data management<title>
          {$y/example}
         </application_example>
```

The role of metadata is pretty obvious: metadata embodies information, which can not be inferred directly from the data. In our e-learning scenario, information about the learning objects, keywords, and the required pre-requisites are not available in the documents themselves, but can be derived from the metadata. Furthermore, you can derive how long it takes a user to learn different modules and how difficult these modules are because this information is specified in the metadata. It is much easier to query metadata than the documents themself because the metadata are in a uniform format, stored in a structured way whereas documents can be heterogeneous and unstructured. All in all, there are two main purposes of metadata in terms of queries:

- specific information can be stored and therefore also queried: information which is not part of the document itself

– information which is kept within the document is easier to query because this information (which is implicit contained in the document) is stored in a structured way in the metadata.

6 Evolution of Federated Information Systems

Information often underlies changes, the amount of available information permanently grows and the formats of the information often modifies. Short-lived data and information often occur in the WWW and accordingly also in federated information systems (FIS). Every FIS has to consider this fact. Some typical evolution steps of a FIS are: (1) addition of data sources (2) changes of the format of data and (3) changes of the metadata format. We now want to consider, which tasks are required if these enumerated evolution steps occur.

1. *Addition of data sources* requires - according to our metadata-based approach - the provision of a metainformation base populated with metadata. Most kinds of metadata have to be added by the user manually because these metadata are not contained in either the data or the documents. The automatic derivation of such metadata that is implicitly contained in the data/documents is supported by the application of specialized methods like:
   - methods based on wrappers ([14], [15], [16]) to analyse documents with a uniform layout.
   - linguistic and ontology based methods ([10], [16]) to analyse documents that belong to the same (restricted) domain.
   Both methods only work for a few kinds of metadata and for very restricted domains. To ensure the quality of these metadata a semiautomatic approach (whereby the user corrects and completes the derived metadata) is better suited than an automatic approach. Within the context of federated information systems the addition of new data sources - with schemas (or schemaelements) previously not included within the global schema - would force the construction of a new global schema, if the new schema elements should be accessible by users. Typically the definition of a global schema reflects the needs of users and applications. These needs are still the same - even after a new source has been added. Therefore the change of a global schema should not be initiated by the addition of a new data source. We also advocate the usage of LOM-congruent schemas on the metainformation level. In this case the addition of a new source does not impose any problems. If a source is added, whose schema on the metainformation level only conforms to a subset of LOM, then that metainformation source will only be able to answer queries according to that specific subset of LOM.
2. *Changes in the data format* require the stored data to adapt towards the new format. It is then possible to use the same data format but to change the structure of the data or the documents (e.g. relational database $\longrightarrow$ relational database or XML $\longrightarrow$ XML). Information can also be stored in a completely different form (e.g. XML $\longrightarrow$ relational database). There are various methods to handle these cases:

96

- If the structure of a relational database changes then we apply the methods for database evolution (e.g.: alter table ...) which are defined in SQL92 ([6]) and SQL99 ([13]).
- For object oriented databases changes of the database structure are more complicated, [22] depicts solutions for that task.
- A current research topic are explicit changes of the structure of XML documents and the adaptation of these XML documents into a new structure, [18] gives an overview on that task. The evolution of XML documents is also a research topic in the MEFIS project: [23] and [7] enumerate the possible changes that can occur, develop a descriptive language for those changes, discuss the effects of each change and provide an implementation.
- There can be changes in the data format such that documents which had been available as XML are stored in databases. There are several methods for this kind of mapping. [11] enumerates and classifies these methods.
- There are also methods to transform data from databases into XML documents. An overview on this approach can be found in [11].

3. *Changes of the metadata format* should occur very seldom. This is especially true if the metadata being used complies to a standard, since the process within standardisation committees normally requires some time. However if it happens - then an adaptation of the available metadata is necessary. Therefore, a query facility for metadata is needed. Changes to the format of the metadata have to be seen within an architectural context. Usually a change of the metadata is initiated on the metainformation level when metainformation sources start describing the underlying data sources according to a more current version of a metadata standard than the one being used by the mediator. As a consequence there will be a mismatch in which the global schema of the mediator and the schema of an underlying source on the metainformation level will be following two different versions of a shared metadata standard. There are different ways in which this mismatch could be solved. A simple solution would be for the mediator to keep track, which of the underlying metainformation sources supports which version of the standard. The global user could then be enabled to select a view corresponding to a particular version of the metadata standard. According to the user's selection appropriate sources supporting the prefered version of the standard would be queried. This solution would suffer from the drawback that only those sources supporting the same version of the standard would be queried leaving the other sources unnoticed. In order to search all metainformation sources the user would have to select all possible schema versions and thus would have to issue multiple queries. On the other hand the amount of available schema versions should be rather small. In a different approach one could try to specify correspondences between the schema elements on the global and on the metainformation level. If such a specification could be done, one would avoid the drawback of the approach mentioned before.

7 Conclusion and Future Work

In this article, we demonstrated that metadata play an important role in a federated information system (FIS). A FIS that offers metadata for the information has less difficulties to operate with new data formats and with changes of data formats. In this article, we demonstrated these advantages for an e-learning environment. We outlined the important role that the metadata standard for learning objects (LOM) assumes within our e-learning scenario: it establishes a shared vocabulary in a granularity which suffices to characterize our educational materials. Besides that the metadata also helped us to build dependency graphs amongst our learning materials so that necessary prerequisites for a successful learning process can be met. The usage of schemas on the metainformation level which conform to the LOM - metadata standard or a subset thereof, proved to bring a substantial reduction in the effort required to construct the global mediator schema. Recently, the research in the project focused on the automatic derivation of metadata from the documents. Furthermore, methods for the evolution of XML documents have been developed. The mapping of XML to databases and the mapping of database information to XML as prerequisites for federated information systems are analysed and methods therefore are developed in the project. For the future, we also want to research other kinds of metadata which might prove helpful in the context of our e-learning scenario. For example, we could also consider the integration of data sources into our federation, which follow a different metadata standard (like e.g. Dublin Core). Since the LOM standard defines a mapping for the Dublin Core elements onto LOM, such knowledge (=metadata) can help in performing the task of integration or the querying of these sources respectively. Besides directing our attention towards such metadata that has been identified by standardization committees (like e.g. LOM for the description of didactic material), there might be other kinds of metadata whose application might be beneficial within an e-learning context. The discovery of such types will also be a major goal within our future work. Furthermore, we will work within the MEFIS project on query transformations, especially the transformation between database queries (SQL) and XML queries (XQuery) which are necessary to query different data and document formats.

References

1. S. Boag, D. Chamberlin, M.F. Fernandez, D. Florescu, J. Robie, J. Siméon, *XQuery 1.0: An XML Query Language*, www.w3.org/TR/xquery/, Nov. 2002
2. C. Batini, M. Lenzerini, S.B. Navathe, *A Comparative Analysis of Methodologies for Database Schema Integration*, ACM Computing Surveys, Vol.18, No.4, December 1986
3. S. Busse, *Modellkorrespondenzen für die kontinuierliche Entwicklung mediatorbasierter Informationssyteme*, Dissertation Technische Universität Berlin, Logos Verlag, 2002
4. S. Conrad, *Föderierte Datenbanksysteme, Konzepte der Datenintegration*, Springer, 1997

5. S. Busse, R.-D. Kutsche, U. Leser, H. Weber, *Federated Information Systems: Concepts, Terminology and Architectures*, Technical Report 99-9, Technical University of Berlin, April 1999

6. C.J. Date, H. Darwen, *SQL - Der Standard*, Addison Wesley, 1998

7. R. Faust, *Prolog-basierte Modellierung von Format-Evolution*, Master thesis, Universität Rostock, 2001

8. M. Garcia-Solaco, F. Saltor, M. Castellanos, *A Structure Based Schema Integration Methodology*, Proc. of the 11th IEEE Int. Conf. on Data Engineering (ICDE'95), S.505 - 512, IEEE Computer Society Press, 1995

9. IEEE Standards Department, *Draft Standard for Learning Object Metadata*, IEEE P1484.12.1-2002, 15.July 2002

10. M. Klettke, M. Bietz, I. Bruder, A. Heuer, D. Priebe, G. Neumann, M. Becker, J. Bedersdorfer, H. Uszkoreit, A. Mädche, S. Staab, R. Studer, *GETESS - Ontologien, Objektrelationale Datenbanken und Textanalyse als Bausteine einer Semantischen Suchmaschine*, Datenbankspektrum, Nr.1(1), 2001

11. M. Klettke, H. Meyer, *XML und Datenbanken*, dpunkt Verlag, 2002

12. A. Löser, C. Grune, M. Hoffmann, *A didactic model, definitions of learning objects and selection of metadata for an online curriculum*, http://www.cti.ac.at/icl/archive/presentation/loeser.pdf, 2002

13. J. Melton, A.R. Simon, J. Gray, *SQL: 1999 - Understanding Relational Language Components*, Morgan Kaufmann, 2002

14. A. Sahuguet, F. Azavant, *Building light-weight wrappers for legacy Web data sources using W4F*, International Conference on Very Large Databases (VLDB), 1999

15. A. Sahuguet, F. Azavant, *WYSIWYG Web Wrapper Factory (W4F)*, 1999

16. A. Schulz, *Anreicherung von Webseiten um beschreibende Metadaten*, Studienarbeit, Universität Rostock, 2001

17. I. Schmitt, *Schemaintegration für den Entwurf Föderierter Datenbanken*, Dissertation Universität Magdeburg, Infix Verlag, 1998

18. H. Su, D.K. Kramer, E.A. Rundensteiner, *XEM: XML Evolution Management*, Technical Report, Worchester Polytechnic Institute, WPI-CS-TR-02-09, January 2002

19. A. Sheth, J. Larson, *Federated Database Systems for Managing Distributed, Heterogeneous, and Autonomous Databases*, ACM Computing Surveys, Vol.22, No.3, September 1990

20. International Standard, ISO/IEC 13249-2, Information technology - Database languages - SQL Multimedia and Application Packages, Part 2: Full-Text, September 2000

21. S. Spaccapietra, C. Parent, Y. Dupont, *Model Independent Assertions for Integration of Heterogeneous Schemas*, VLDB Journal, 1(1): 81-126, 1992

22. M. Tresch, *Evolution in Datenbanken*, PhD Thesis, Teubner Text zur Mathematik, Band 10, Ulm, September 1994

23. A. Zeitz, *Evolution von XML-Dokumenten*, Studienarbeit, Universität Rostock, 2001

Building platforms
for information system interoperability:
a UML-based metamodeling approach

Marie-Noëlle Terrasse, Marinette Savonnet, Eric Leclercq, and George Becker

Laboratoire LE2I, Université de Bourgogne
B.P. 47870, 21078 Dijon Cedex, France
E-mail: {terrasse,savonnet,leclercq,becker}@khali.u-bourgogne.fr

Abstract. Models already play a major role in information system engineering
and interoperability. This paper emphasizes the complementary role played by
metamodels. Metamodels are used as a core of two innovative platforms for information system interoperability. The first platform allows to combine formal
and informal approaches for both modeling and interoperability of information
systems. The second platform uses metamodeling and reengineering in order to
reuse existing interoperability know-how for the Semantic Web. Both platforms
are based on metamodels obtained by integrating metamodels of participating
information systems. Such integration of metamodels is carried out by using a
UML-based metamodeling architecture that we have proposed.

1   Introduction

Information system engineering is turning into an increasingly complex process which
has to take into account intricacies of information systems, their deployment environments, and users' requirements [17]. Metamodeling has been introduced to cope with
such complexity, with many metamodeling architectures being based on UML (e.g., the
OMG's architecture). UML-based metamodeling environments support a straightforward modeling process: first, describing –by a metamodel– an application domain, and
then instantiating such a metamodel into a model. In order to avoid metamodel prolif-
eration, several authors have proposed to organize UML-based application model descriptions into an inheritance hierarchy [7,9]. Yet, such inheritance hierarchy does not
solve the problem of interoperability. Information system interoperability relies upon
a metamodel as a semantical reference and such a metamodel may not necessarily exist. We illustrate the need of a semantical reference on the following example in the
context of geographic information systems. Figure 1 presents segments of content of
cross-domain descriptions which are related to time and space: metamodel-components,
model-components, and instance-components.

First, let us assume that all the metamodels under consideration refer to the same
time description. Thus, a common semantics for time exists and it can be described
by an integrated metamodel. In such a case, cross-domain descriptions are based upon
the integrated metamodel: transformation tools can be limited to model and instance

	TIME: a unique time semantics		SPACE: two universes of the discourse	
			Earth space	Galactic space
Metamodel level	Integrated metamodel		metamodel translation ⟷	
			Earth-space metamodel	Galactic-space metamodel
Model level	model translation ⟷		model translation ⟷	
	date	interval	Clark, UTM, Lambert, etc.	equatorial coordinates
Instance level	unit translation ⟷		unit translation ⟷	
	hour	year	km	light-year
	reference translation ⟷		reference translation ⟷	
	Hijra era	Christian era	Lambert I,IV	B1950.0, J2000.0

Fig. 1. On the role of metamodels in information systems interoperability

levels. Thus, semantical integrity of answers to user-queries is guaranteed by the integrated metamodel. Second, let us assume that metamodels under consideration refer to different space descriptions (i.e., Earth space and Galactic space), and that there is no integrated metamodel for space. In such a case, cross-domain descriptions need to provide information systems with transformation tools for space description at the metamodel, model and instance levels. Also, some of the answers to user-queries depend on transformation tool accuracy: the global system has no semantics of its own for space.

Based upon the above discussion, it is clear that federated information systems need to have their semantics, if it exists, expressed in terms of a specific metamodel. We have developed a UML-based metamodeling architecture in which we provide semi-formal operations on metamodels: metamodel integration and a measure of a semantical distance between metamodels [19, 20]. We are convinced that our metamodeling architecture is suitable for building a semantical basis –in the form of an integrated metamodel– for various kinds of information system interoperability. Section 2 describes two example platforms built on integrated metamodels. Section 3 presents our ongoing work.

2   Two example platforms based on integrated metamodels

In our architecture, a metamodel is described by two sets: a set of UML constructs and a set of OCL constraints. An integration of two given metamodels is achieved by a union-like operation on their sets of constructs and a union-like operation on their sets of constraints (see [20] for details). As an example of metamodel integration, let us first describe a metamodel which corresponds to the UWE project's modeling paradigm for hypermedia [13]. Such an extension consists of additional diagrams[1] and stereotypes needed for those diagrams[2]. A second metamodel which corresponds to the modeling paradigm of Fröhlich & al. [10] for hypermedia offers diagrams similar to those of Koch & al. [13]. There are more explicit restrictions in Fröhlich & al. metamodel: a restriction to binary associations, and an inter-diagram constraint in order to limit possible types of navigation in the associated navigational structure model. A third metamodel corresponds to the modeling paradigm of Alatalo & al. [1] for mobile-aware hypermedia (OWLA project). The authors introduce a stereotype of association, denoted by ≪CondAssociation≫, in order to discriminate *conditional associations* (whose corresponding links have guarded navigability depending on users's location) from *unconditional associations*. Integration of Fröhlich & al. and Alatalo & al.'s metamodels produces a metamodel which encompasses: 1) constructs of UWE project's metamodel, and the ≪CondAssociation≫ stereotype; 2) constraints of UWE project's metamodel, restriction to binary associations, and restriction of possible types of navigation (specified in the associated navigational structure model) depending on multiplicities of associations in the navigational space model.

In this section we propose two platforms based on such integrated metamodels. In our first plateform, integrated metamodels form the core of a toolbox for interoperability of information systems. In the second plateform, integrated metamodels form the basis for cross-domain descriptions built bottom-up.

2.1 A platform for modeling and interoperability of information systems

Modeling environments inherently evolve towards integration of formal methods with programming tools. As depicted in Figure 2 (light-grey thick arrows), such environments propose: a *core component* for elaboration of metamodels[3], models and their documentations; a *specification toolbox* for production of a correct specification[4]; and a *programming toolbox* for generation and testing of executable code from such a specification. In order to extend the same approach to interoperability, we propose the following additional components (see dark-grey thick arrows in Figure 2): a formal interoperability toolbox and an agreement toolbox. A *formal interoperability toolbox* produces an abstract basis of agreement from a set of specifications of interoperating information systems. Such an abstract basis of agreement is produced in terms of a metamodel (by using our metamodel integration). An *agreement toolbox* generates concrete bases of agreement from abstract bases of agreement. We propose to use abstract bases of agreement in the same way Gruber [11] uses *ontologies of representation* (ontologies which capture representation primitives but do not define their content). Defining the

---

[1] A *navigational space model* describes classes that users are allowed to visit, together with links available for navigation between these classes. A *navigational structure model* describes which types of navigation are available for each link (guided tour, index, etc.). A *static presentational model* describes how objects are presented to users (i.e., interfaces), etc.

[2] Stereotypes of class: ≪*navigational class*≫, ≪*guided tour*≫, etc.

[3] See Clark & al.'s proposal [5].

[4] By using formal validation of models [6, 16], validation of models against user requirements [3, 8, 12], test generation [2, 15], etc.

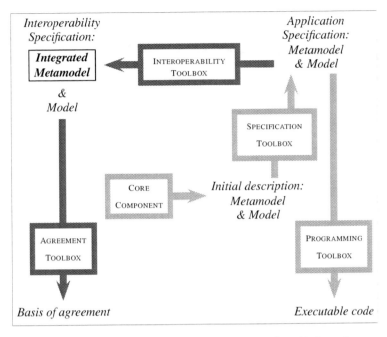

Fig. 2. An integrated platform for modeling and interoperability of information systems

content of the concrete basis of agreement is a process similar to the instantiation of a metamodel into a model.

2.2 A platform for the Semantic Web

We propose a platform for the Semantic Web which enables reuse of know-how that has been already established and refined for interoperability. Our metamodeling architecture can be used as a basis of a new approach to the Semantic Web development in which: each domain is described by a domain library containing both metamodels and models, while narrowly focused domain descriptions can be integrated for cross-domain applications. The platform we propose encompasses the following processes depicted in Figure 3: an *attachment process* establishes a dependency between a web-enabled information system and its metamodel taken from a library of domain descriptions. The assumption of existence of such a referring metamodel for any web-enabled system might appear rather restrictive. Yet due to the development of UML as a standard tool for high-level system descriptions[5], this assumption is reasonable (or will soon become reasonable). Our *reengineering process* is a reversal of Koch's hypermedia UML-based modeling methods [14]. The reengineering process collects a representative sample of navigation paths and then expresses them as a web data-model of the information system. An *integration process* produces an integrated metamodel from which the cross-domain description can be built. In this way, we permit a semantic search to be car-

---

[5] See, for example, OMG's profiles [18], Cook's prefaces [7], and UML-based ontologies [4].

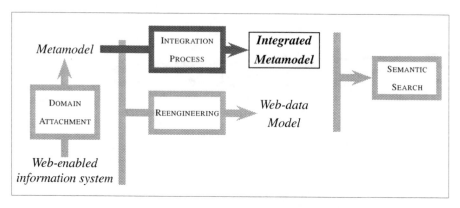

Fig. 3. Our platform for the Semantic Web

ried out based on a sound semantical reference (which is defined at the model and metamodel levels, i.e, by the web data-models and their corresponding integrated meta-model, respectively).

3 Conclusion

We have proposed a metamodeling architecture which takes advantage of knowledge of modelers' behavior, abstract approaches to modeling of information systems, and formal methods. Metamodels –which implement abstraction mechanisms– form the core of our architecture. Our metamodel integration, which we have defined in the context of such a metamodeling architecture, is used as a basis for innovative frameworks in information system engineering and the Semantic Web. We continue our work on several technical aspects of this project. First, we seek to define a convenient interface for using our metamodeling structure in the form of a library of domain descriptions. Second, we need to precisely define which functionalities are expected from agreement toolboxes (for generation of concrete bases of agreement from abstract bases of agreement). Third, we need to define an attachment process for our platform for the Semantic Web.

We believe that extensive use of our proposal would open a "standardization" issue, namely the need for a new organization of domain modeling. Modelers would be responsible for "local semantics" (i.e., for describing their own application domain as a variation of an existing domain description). Domain experts would be responsible for global semantics (i.e., for validating semantical dependencies between domain descriptions).

References

1. T. Alatalo and J. Peraho. Designing Mobile-aware Adaptive Hypermedia. In *Proc. of the Third Workshop on Adaptive Hypertext and Hypermedia*, 2001.
2. P. Ammann and P. E. Black. Abstracting Formal Specifications to Generate Software Tests via Model Checking. In *Proc. of the 18th Digital Avionics Systems Conference, DASC'99, Saint Louis, Missouri, USA*, 1999. Available at URL www.nist.gov.

3. K. Androutsopoulos. The Reactive System Development Support Tool. Technical report, King's College, Department of Computing, 1999. Available at URL http://www.dcs.kcl.ac.uk/pg/kelly.

4. K. Baclawski, M.Kokar, P. Kogut, L. Hart, J. Smith, W. Holmes, J. Letkowski, and M. Aronson. Extending UML to Support Ontology Engineering for the Semantic Web. In *Proc. of the International Conference on UML, UML'01, Toronto, Canada*, 2001.

5. T. Clark, A. Evans, S. Kent, and P. Sammut. The MMF Approach to Engineering Object-Oriented Design Languages. In *Proc. of the Workshop on language, descriptions, Tools and Applications, LDTA01*, 2001.

6. E. M. Clarke and J. M. Wing. Formal Methods: State of Art and Future Directions. In *ACM Computing Surveys*, 28(4), pages 626–643. ACM, December 1996.

7. S. Cook, A. Kleppe, R. Mitchell, B. Rumpe, J. Warmer, and A. C. Wills. Defining UML Family Members Using Prefaces. In C. Mingins and B. Meyer, editors, *Proc. of "Technology of Object-Oriented Languages and Systems", TOOLS 32*, pages 102–114. IEEE, 1999.

8. A. Daskalopulu. Model Checking Contractual Protocols. In *Proc. of the 13th Annual Conference JURIX'2000*, pages 35–47, 2000.

9. E. D. Falkenberg and J.L. Han Oei. Meta Model Hierarchies from an Object-Role Modeling Perspective. In *Proc. of the 1st International Conference on Object-Role Modeling, ORM-1, Magnetic Island, Australia*, 1994.

10. P. Frohlich, N. Henze, and W. Nejdl. Meta-Modeling for Hypermedia Design. In *Proceedings of the Second IEEE Metadata Conference, MD97*, 1997.

11. T. Gruber. A Translation Approach to Portable Ontology Specification. *Knowledge Acquisition*, 5:199–220, 1993.

12. R. D. Jeffords and C. Heitmeyer. An Algorithm for Strengthening State Invariants Generated from Requirements Specifications. In *Proc. of the 5th International Symposium on Requirements Engineering, RE'01*, Toronto, Canada, August 2001. IEEE.

13. N. Koch, H. Baumeister, R. Hennicker, and L. Mandel. Extending UML for Modeling Navigation and Presentation in Web Applications. In *Proc. of the Workshop Modeling Web Applications in the UML, UML'00*, 2000.

14. N. Koch and M. Wirsing. Software Engineering for Adaptative Hypermedia Applications. In *Proc. of the 8th International Conference on User Modeling, Sonthofen, Germany*, 2001.

15. B. Legeard and F. Peureux. Automatic Generation of Functional Test Sequences from B Formal Specifications - Presentation and Industrial Case Study. In *Proc. of the 16th IEEE Conference on Automated Software Engineering, ASE'2001*, 2001.

16. I. Ober. Difficulties in Defining Precise Semantics for UML. ECOOP'00 Workshop 14 on Defining a Precise Semantics for UML, Sophia Antipolis, France, June 2000.

17. UML4MDA, Response to the OMG RFP Infrastructure for UML2.0, Report 2003-01-13. Available at URL http://www.omg.org, January 2003.

18. A UML Profile for CORBA, OMG Report 99-08-02. Version 1.0, August 2, 1999.

19. M.-N. Terrasse. A Metamodeling Approach to Evolution. In H. Balsters, B. de Bruck, and S. Conrad, editors, *Database Schema Evolution and Meta-Modeling*. Springer-Verlag, LNCS 2065, ISBN 3-540-42272-2, 2001. 9th International Workshop on Foundations of Models and Languages for Data and Objects, Schloss Dagstuhl, Germany, 2000.

20. M.-N. Terrasse, M. Savonnet, and G. Becker. An UML-metamodeling Architecture for Interoperability of Information Systems. In *Proc. of the International Conference on Information Systems Modelling, ISM'01*, 2001.

Designing Roles For Object-Relational Databases*

Ling Wang and Mark Roantree

Interoperable Systems Group, Dublin City University, Ireland
{lwang,mark}@computing.dcu.ie

Abstract. The concept of 'role' views have been studied in software engineering and database research areas for a number of years and the concepts are now well understood. Similarly, the deployment of view mechanisms for both relational and object-oriented data models is familiar to most database researchers. The need for a semantically powerful view mechanism in federated architectures is also agreed by most data researchers. As the popularity of the standard object model (ODMG) continues to drop, and the object-relational model gains acceptance, research should now focus on the development of semantically powerful view mechanisms for the newer model. Furthermore, the availability of real object-relational technologies such as Oracle 9i offers researchers the opportunity to develop different forms of view mechanisms. This research describes the deployment of a role-based view system for Object-Relational databases. It provides a new look at an alternate view mechanism, based on the object-relational industry standard.

1 Introduction

The concept of federated database systems is where heterogeneous databases can communicate with each other through an interface provided by a canonical data model. In many federated database research projects an object-oriented model (and often the ODMG model) was selected as canonical model. However due to the lack of popularity of the ODMG model and the emergence of stronger object-relational models (Oracle 9i for example), there are now genuine options for canonical models using the original criteria for canonical model selection [8]. Furthermore, it provides an opportunity to develop a new view mechanism as the current object-relational standard provides a mechanism for defining virtual tables only. (Note: In this research, we regard the latest version of Oracle to be the object-relational standard.) In a federated database system, views should retain as much semantic information as possible, a property that aids the subsequent integration operations. The focus of this paper is the deployment of localized role views: the integration aspect is part of current research.

The structure of this paper is as follows: in the remainder of this section, background and motivation are provided. §2 describes related work in this area.

---

* Supported by Enterprise Ireland Strategic Grant IF/2001/305.

§3 presents a full specification of the language needed for usage. §4 presents operations for restructuring roles, and finally, §5 provides conclusions.

1.1 Background and Motivation

The IOMPAR project [7] is a funded collaboration between Dublin City University and a number of industrial partners including Iona Technologies. Its aims are to offer a secure transfer of textual and non-textual data between data sources operating in a federated database architecture. Databases require restructuring capabilities for complex objects to cope with different representations of real-world entities. In a federated database architecture, it is necessary for each participating system to provide a description (view definition) of its shareable data in a semantically rich manner. While the OR model may provide the semantic power for canonical model requirements, the restructuring functionality is provided by using OR views. In our opinion, the current mechanism for defining views is not sufficient to support powerful localized views. The motivation of this research is two-fold: to examine the deployment of the latest Oracle model (both as a model and metamodel) as a federated canonical model, and to specify and implement a view mechanism which is more powerful than that currently offered.

Contribution.

In the context of the IOMPAR project, this research task does not address integration issues but focuses on the provision of view classes for the object-relational model. Specifically we require: support for object migration, multiple instantiation of the same class occurrences and context-dependent access. These features have been identified in the study of *role concepts* in the OO literature [3]. In this context, our approach offers an alternative to traditional view systems. In a study of the Oracle 9i metamodel to determine its suitability for including model role concepts [10], we suggested extensions to the OR metamodel to support root and roles. Our contribution is the provision (specification and implementation) of a new view mechanism for the object-relational model. Specifically, an extended Structured Query Language (SQL-99) [5] is used to provide the specifications and mappings to support restructuring, and to generate extents for the virtual classes in role views.

2 Related Work

In this section, we examine some recent proposals which present roles in practice and define their own view mechanisms with the association of roles. Each proposal with relation to the following criteria: the contributions and the limitations, the context of roles and views (if present) and the beneficial features that we may reuse.

2.1 Extended Smalltalk

Extended SmallTalk [4] focuses on defining new objects with role extensions in OO databases. The authors relax some restrictions that traditional OO model cannot manage, such as dynamically changing object type and context-access. The contribution of this work is that multiple occurrences of the same class is enabled by defining a new type `QualifiedRoleType`. The extended language supports creating objects based on the role concept rather than implementing this concept with the current OO model. In other words, a view mechanism is not a relevant issue in this proposal. Conversely, our focus is on how to restructure or review the defined objects, which have been stored in OR databases. At the cost-saving point, this is better approach than redefining all the objects in the schema. Although this proposal resolves many issues that the traditional OO model presents, it is based on a single individual object. We concentrate on generating collection of objects with the capability of restructuring each object in the role view. Also this proposal asserts that a role may play another role, which causes many ambiguities. We remove this conflict by allowing only the root to plays roles. We use the term of `multirole` to address the issue that `QualifiedRoleType` resolved.

2.2 DOOR/MM

The three contributions in DOOR/MM [12] are supporting object migration; extending multimedia object with the notion of roles; and integrating views and roles. In this project, multimedia objects are the target rather than plain text based objects. In this proposal, views are modeled as multiple representations and abstractions of a multimedia object, and roles as an object-based specialization of a multimedia object for dynamic extension, as well as integrating the heterogeneous types of information in OO model. In other words, objects and roles (but not views) are regarded as logical entities, and views are regarded as presentations of these logical entities [12]. A view is specified as a virtual role of an object, whereas we regard a view as a wrapper of logical objects. Although the authors claim that a view may be defined by extracting the abstract and references from other views to represent multifaceted features of multimedia object, there is no prototype or implementation supported. We differ from this approach by providing a role-based virtual schema which contains as much semantic information as possible, rather than just a phenomenon of single role. In this proposal, roles and views are defined with no capability of restructuring. We use SQL-99 [5] to present some restructuring of role classes.

2.3 Galileo

This proposal focuses on developing views for OO databases with the semantics of viewing operations in a language that supports objects with role concept [2]. Views are defined as virtual objects while other approaches work by defining virtual classes. Authors state that roles and views are common since they both

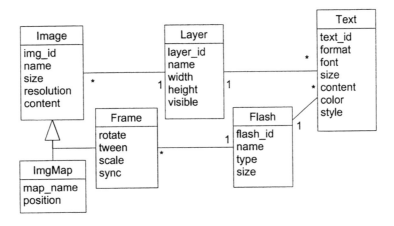

Fig. 1. Website Design Schema

allow an object to be extended. The contribution of this proposal is the clarification of the relationship between roles and views, the different semantics of method overriding and evaluation in views and roles. Although some view operations are specified in this proposal, which presents more flexibility than in proposal *2.2*, the view is still based on one single object rather than a collection of objects. Furthermore, the premise of defining a view is that the object has to be well specified with role extensions. In other words, if the stored object is not modeled by object-role format, a view of that object cannot be implemented and view operators have no use. We differ because we chose a single complex model upon which to base role views.

3 Object-Relational Roles in IOMPAR

In IOMPAR, we assume that roles have the following characteristics: a root may play multiple roles or the same multiple times; a role belongs to a single root; a role cannot exist without its root; deleting a root implies deleting all of its roles. An introduction to roles are provided in the full version of this paper [11].

3.1 Definition Language Syntax

We now provide a syntax for defining role views. The extended SQL definition language is presented in this section by illustrating the more important aspects. The role view definition starts with retrieving the structure of underlying UDTs with the *projection* option. There are two options for generating the extents for root and role classes, which are either retrieve the entire extent of the underlying UDT or to select only subset of the extent with the **where** option. Since we concentrate on defining the role view structure at this section, the root and role

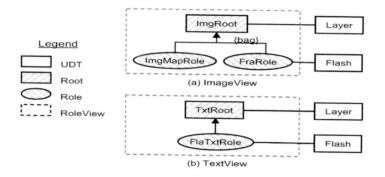

Fig. 2. Role Samples

extents simply are generated by retrieving the entire extents of based UDTs. A full discussion on extents is provided in *section 3.2*.

The formal role syntax is expressed in BNF format in the appendix of the full paper [11]. In this section, examples are used to introduce the syntax in a less formal manner. All examples present the definition for the role view illustrated in *figure 2*, which is based on the schema presented in *figure 1*.

Example 1. ImageView Definition.
```
create roleview ImageView as
root ImgRoot of Image is (
          select *
          from Image_ObjTab)
role ImgMapRole of ImageMap is (
          select map_name, position
          from ImgMap_ObjTab),
multirole FraRole of Frame is (
          select rotate,tween,fla_ref
          from Frame_ObjTab);
```

In *example 1*, `ImageView` defines one root `ImgRoot` and the two roles `ImgMapRole` and `FraRole`. The latter is a `multirole` where multiple occurrences are allowed. The appropriate properties are easily retrieved from the metadata repository, with new role metadata generated and stored in the extended Oracle repository. `ImgRoot`, `ImgMapRole` and `FraRole` are based on previously defined UDTs, and `ImgMapRole` and `FraRole` are restructured using the *projection* option.

The previous example illustrates that the root and roles may be based on different UDTs. However, it is also possible for the root and roles to be based on a single UDT provided that attribute sets are disjoint. In *example 2*, we assume that when a `Text` object links to a `Flash` object, it actually plays a temporary role as flash text. The attribute `flash_ref` indicates the association between the `Flash` and `Text` objects. The `layer_ref` association provides the link between the `Layer` and `Text` objects.

Example 2. TextView Definition.

```
create roleview TextView as
root TxtRoot of Text is (
        select text_id,format,font,size,layer_ref
        from Text_ObjTab)
role FlaTxtRole of Text is (
        select color,style,flash_ref
        from Text_ObjTab);
```

In a real world scenario, it is possible that an object exists only with its intrinsic properties and acquires a transient role afterward. A typical example is where a person becomes an employee at some point in time. Thus, it is possible to define a role view with a root but no role specification and later redefine the view with role classes. We make the following assumptions about the role view definition: the object table of a root or role based UDT exists in the database schema; no nested `select` statement is contained in the definition; the defined role view is a multi-set.

3.2 Generating Extents for Roles

The next step is to generate extents for role view classes with the **where** option using the UDTs on which they are based. The **where** clause in SQL is used to filter the objects and the root and role class extents are generated as the result. If no **where** clause is specified (*example 1 & 2*), then the entire extents for the underlying UDTs are added to the extents of the role classes. *Example 3* generates the specific extent of the role view from *example 1*.

Example 3. ImageView Definition with Extent.

```
create roleview ImageView as
root ImgRoot of Image is (
        select *
        from Image_ObjTab
        where name = 'Fischár')
role ImgMapRole of ImageMap is (
        select map_name, position
        from ImgMap_ObjTab
        where position = 'north' or map_name = 'dcu_ban'),
multirole FraRole of Frame is (
        select rotate,tween,fla_ref
        from Frame_ObjTab
        where tween != 'shape');
```

Figure 3 illustrates how the extents of root and role classes are generated in *example 3*. The non-shaded columns and rows are not part of the view specification, and the `multirole` FraRole {auto,motion} is represented using two rows. Thus, there are two objects in the `ImgRoot` class (which gets its extent from the Oracle `Image_ObjTab` table) and one object in the `FraRole` class. These three objects are part of the root extent by default.

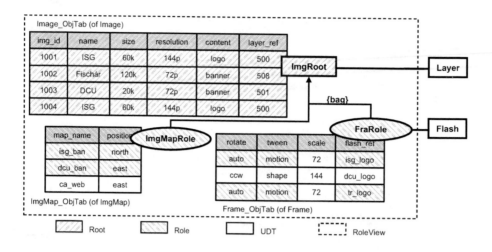

Fig. 3. ImageView with Extents

- **ImgRoot** extent: according to the root specification, only the image named as "Fischár" is selected as root object. When a **where** predicate is used in the root definition, it implies that those objects selected play no current roles. In our current version, it is the responsibility of the user to ensure that this selection does not overlap with role extents as it is specifically used to identify those objects which are required for the role view although they do not currently play a role.
- **ImgMapRole** extent: The role extent contains the two **ImageMap** objects which satisfy the **where** predicate. It is permitted for role extents to overlap as some entities can play two roles simultaneously.
- **FraRole** extent: instead of single role specification, **FraRole** is specified as a **multirole** which supports multiple occurrences. With the **multirole** feature, a one-to-many relationship is created between the root and the **FraRole** role.

A root and role may be based on a single UDT. *Example 4* expands the definition shown in *example 2* with a **where** option, and *figure 4* illustrates the result.

Example 4. TextView Definition with Extent.
```
    create roleview TextView as
    root TxtRoot of Text is (
            select text_id,format,font,size,layer_ref
            from Text_ObjTab
            where text_id = '2002')
    role FlaTxtRole of Text is (
            select color,style,flash_ref
            from Text_ObjTab
            where color = 'FF6600' and flash_ref = 'isg_logo'
```

```
or flash_ref = 'tr_logo');
```

The `Text` extent is divided into `TxtRoot` extent and `FlaTxtRole` extent. According to the root specification, there is one `Text` object is selected as the root object. According to the role specification, there are two `Text` objects are selected into the role extent. As stated previously, these two objects are part of the root extent by default. The root object `Text` "2002" does not play role `FlaTxtRole` currently; hence there are three root objects in the root extent.

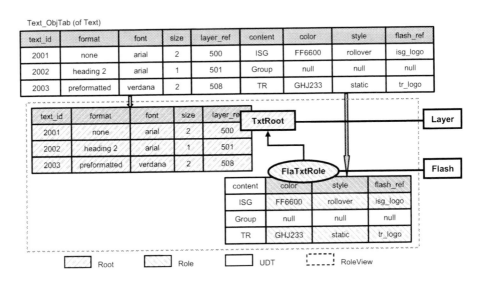

Fig. 4. TextView with Extents

To summarize our approach to generating extents for classes in role views: each role class has its extent specified by the `where` clause in the role specification, while the root extent is generating using both the `where` clause for the root, together with an aggregation of extents for all roles.

While generating extents, an object preserving semantics is used for root objects in order that they retain the same identifiers as their underlying UDTs. As we do not support a *join* operation in this version, this removes any ambiguities regarding updates. However, an object generating semantics is employed for role objects so that each role has a unique (but transient) identifier. This is in line with traditional role based concepts.

4 Role View Operations

Operators are provided that modify the structure or manipulate the extents. The `add` and `drop` operators are used to restructure the defined classes in SQL-99 [5].

We modify these operators and allow them to modify the root and role classes. Some new operators are defined for manipulating role objects, such as `acquire`, `abandon` and `migrate`. The BNF expressions of each operator is contained in the appendix of the full paper [11].

Example 5 illustrates how `add` and `drop` operators are implemented. The `alter` operator is used to emphasize the alteration of a role view. The `add` operator addresses the operation of adding one or more new properties; and the `drop` operator addresses the operation of removing one or more properties from the current root or role classes.

Example 5. Modify Root or Role.
```
(a) alter roleview ImageView
       add attribute fileType to root ImgRoot;

(b) alter roleview ImageView
       drop attribute tween, scale from role FraRole;
```
As *example 5(a)* shows, the `fileType` attribute is retrieved from the underlying UDT's object table. Since it is taken from the same UDT the `from` clause is not necessary. In *example 5(b)*, the property `tween` and `scale` are dropped from a role class.

4.1 Acquire Operator

The `acquire` operator is used to update a role extent by placing a new object into a role extent (and root extent by default).

Example 6. Root Object Acquire Role Object.
```
acquire role ImgMapRole
from roleview ImageView
where root ImgRoot.img_id = '1003';
```

It is also possible to acquire a new multi-role by using the `acquire multirole` command.

4.2 Abandon Operator

The `abandon` operator is used to drop a role. It is not possible to drop a root object: this is achieved when it is removed from the underlying UDT.

Example 7. Abandon Role Object from Root Object.
```
abandon role ImgMapRole
from roleview ImageView
where root ImgRoot.img_id = '1003';
```

Again, there are two important conditions that guarantee this operation succeeds: the root "1003" exists in the root extent; and it definitely has an `ImgMap` role. Otherwise, an error message will be generated.

114

4.3 Migrate Operator

The `Migrate` operator permits the changing of a root object while retaining all role information. Under normal circumstances this requires a number of operations to delete all root and role data, and then add new root and role data. This is not necessary where a new object 'replaces' an existing one.

Example 8. Migrate Role Object.
```
migrate role ImgMapRole
from roleview ImageView
where ImgRoot.name = 'ISG'
to ImgRoot.name = 'DCU';
```

5 Conclusions and Future Work

In this paper the deployment of a role-based view system for the object-relational model was presented. This has been implemented using Oracle 9i for storage and Java and ANTLR [1] for development and parsing operations. To build this system it was first necessary to analyze and then extend the Oracle 9i metamodel. This work required the addition of new meta-tables to the schema repository and is described fully in [9]. While OR meta-tables do not physically exist[1], it was necessary for our mechanism to place a number of 'virtual' UDTs into the Oracle database. A full description of these tables can be found in [10]. Access to the extended Oracle repository is provided by the IOMPAR metadata service [6]. Extended SQL-99 is used to define role views, and a Java-ANTLR processor parses role specifications and stores role metadata in the virtual UDTs. A View Display system uses the methodology for extents (described in §3.2) to display role views.

Our present work is focused on the extension of the role view system to facilitate various integration operations to allow the system to combine roles from separate databases.

References

1. ANTLR, Complete Language Translation Solutions. jGuru, 2003.
2. A. Albanoand, A. Antognoni, and G. Ghelli. View Operations on Objects with Roles for a Statically Typed Database Language. *Knowledge and Data Engineering*, 12(4):548–567, 2000.
3. M. Dahchour, A. Pirotte, and E. Zimányi. A Generic Role Model for Dynamic Objects. In *The 14th Advanced Information Systems Engineering nternational Conference, CAiSE'02*, Toronto, Canada, May 27-31, 2002.
4. G. Gottlob, M. Schrefl, and B. Röck. Extending Object-Oriented Systems with Roles. *ACM Transactions on Information Systems*, 14(3):268–296, 1996.
5. P. Gulutzan and T. Pelzer. *SQL-99 Complete, Really An Example-Based Reference Manual of the New Standard.* R&D Books Miller Freeman, Inc., 1999.

---

[1] Oracle constructs view metatables dynamically.

6. G. O'Connor. A Metadata Interface to Access Extended O-R Meta-Information. Technical Report ISG-02-13, Dublin City University, Glasnevin, Dublin 9, Ireland, December 2003.

7. M. Roantree. Metadata Management in Federated Multimedia Databases. In *The 13th Australian Databases Conference ADC'02*, pages 263–276, Melbourne, Australia, January 2002.

8. F. Saltor, M. Castellanos, and M. García-Solaco. Suitability of Data Model as Canonical Models for Federated Databases. *ACM SIGMOD Record*, 1991.

9. L. Wang. An Analysis of Object-Relational Model. Technical Report ISG-02-06, Dublin City University, Glasnevin, Dublin 9, Ireland, 2002.

10. L. Wang. Extending the Object-Relational Metamodel to Facilitate the Definition of Roles. Technical Report ISG-02-11, Dublin City University, Glasnevin, Dublin 9, Ireland, October 2002.

11. L. Wang. Designing Roles for Object-Relational Databases. Technical Report ISG-03-02, Dublin City University, Glasnevin Dublin 9, 2003.

12. R.K. Wong. Heterogeneous and Multifaceted Multimedia Objects in DOOR/MM: A Roles-Based Approach with Views. *Parallel and Distributed Computing*, 56:235–250, November 1998.

Intrinsic Support for Metadata Integration in Relational Federations

Catharine M. Wyss[1], James J. Lu[2], Shun Yan Cheung[2], and
Mehdi M. Akhavein[2]

[1] Department of Computer Science and School of Informatics, Indiana University,
Bloomington, IN 47405-7104 crood@cs.indiana.edu
[2] Department of Mathematics and Computer Science, Emory University, Atlanta, GA 30322
jlu,cheung,makhave@mathcs.emory.edu

Abstract. This paper investigates the idea of supporting metadata querying and restructuring using extensions of the SQL:1999 facilities for integrity constraints and active databases. Our approach involves associating *meta-functionality* with federation relations by means of constraints, assertions, and triggers. This approach can underpin recent work on dynamic interoperability in relational federations involving an extended relational model. An advantage of the approach described here is that it provides intrinsic, database-driven support for dynamic restructuring and federated interoperability. A drawback is that, if not developed properly, the extended notions of constraints, assertions, and triggers can exacerbate existing issues with the practical efficiency of database-driven integrity support. We discuss this trade-off, and conclude with a brief indication of how our work fits in to existing work and some directions for future work.

1 Introduction

The strength of a Federated Information System can arguably be measured by its ability to perform automatic, dynamic restructuring of the data sources comprising the federation. Such restructuring is the hallmark of a flexible, useful system for managing heterogeneous data from disparate sources, and is crucial for architectures defining a common data model and/or common query language through which accesses to all constituent data take place. In a federation comprised of relational sources, for example, the dominant architecture is *wrapper-based* and involves the creation of special-purpose wrappers for translating global data manipulation into locally manifested operations [5].

A recent extension of SQL has been proposed that facilitates the automatic creation and maintenance of wrapper-based FIS architectures for relational federations [10, 9]. The extended language, FISQL (Federated Interoperable SQL) allows real-time dynamic restructuring through operationalization using an extended relational algebra [11]. As a next step in providing realized, automatic dynamic restructuring capabilities to relational federations, our work has focused on implementing the FISQL/FIRA framework as an add-on to existing relational platforms. While procedural extensions supporting metadata querying and restructuring (for example using the SQL CLI) may prove to be more feasible, declarative extensions to SQL:1999 supporting dynamic restructuring have nonetheless proved interesting and, in some ways, more natural.

In this paper, we investigate extending the SQL:1999 support for integrity constraints and active databases to encompass intrinsic support for metadata querying and restructuring in a relational federation. We term this extended RDBMS framework the *Meta*-RDBMS or MRDBMS framework. An over-arching goal of our work is to support uniform, automatic creation and maintenance of wrappers, mediating views, and metadata repositories for FIS. Recently, our work on MRDBMSs has expanded to include semi-structured data as a natural extension of the MRDBMS idea of *meta-functionality*. In this paper, we consider attaching meta-functionality to relational tables; this meta-functionality could rather be seen as attaching to relational datatypes, in which case several interesting parallels with XML Schemas emerge [2].

2 Overview of the MRDBMS Framework

Current relational database management systems (RDBMS) manage metadata using system-specific tables. The *Meta-Relational DBMS* (MRDBMS) framework extends this idea with mechanisms for encoding the semantics of user-specified metadata. Specifically, meta-functionality is attached to relations through two extensions of SQL:1999.

- Triggers which specifically induce meta-properties of the data in the relation (we call these MTRIGGERs); and
- Constraints which encode semantic properties arising from meta-properties. These will be of two types: MCONSTRAINTs (single-relation constraints) and MASSERTIONs (multiple relation and/or globally applicable constraints).

Thus, meta-relations contain ordinary data having associated with it functionality which distinguishes it as *metadata* (i.e. *meta-functionality*). On this view, canonical relations are simply meta-relations having *no* associated meta-functionality. The following sections serve to indicate the breadth of application of this idea.

2.1 Schema Management

Consider a relation schema having the following SQL:1999 declaration:

```
CREATE TABLE schema AS
     ( db_name  STRING NOT NULL,
       rel_name STRING NOT NULL,
       att_name STRING NOT NULL,
       att_type STRING NOT NULL,
       col_ID   AUTONUMBER,
       CONSTRAINT schema_pk PRIMARY KEY (col_ID),
       CONSTRAINT schema_ck UNIQUE (db_name, rel_name) );
```

The intent is that this table explicitly represents the schema of the federation. Each relation in the federation has a unique pathname of the form db_name::rel_name. Furthermore, every column can be referenced by the primary key col_ID, which is an automatically generated identifier. Informally, the col_ID value will stay the same, even if the name of the referenced column changes (for example on a schema update).

The intention of the schema relation is to mimic behavior of RDBMS by having this table explicitly represent the schema definitions. To achieve this purpose, we attach meta-triggers (MTRIGGERs) to table schema, as discussed in the next sections.

Schema Insertion In order that relation schema maintains the number and shape of relations in our federation, tuples inserted in the schema relation have the side-effect of creating new tables (or altering existing ones). Thus, we have an MTRIGGER realize_insert that "realizes" the inserted metadata in terms of database objects.

```
CREATE MTRIGGER realize_insert AFTER INSERT ON schema
FOR EACH ROW
BEGIN
    IF ( EXISTS ( SELECT *
                  FROM    schema S
                  WHERE S.db_name = new.db_name AND
                        S.rel_name = new.rel_name ) )
        /* alter existing table */
        ALTER TABLE new.db_name::new.rel_name
           ADD COLUMN new.att_name new.att_type;
    ELSE
        /* create new table */
        CREATE TABLE new.db_name::new.rel_name
           (new.att_name new.type);
END;
```

Schema Deletion Similarly, we would need to handle the case of deletion from the schema relation by deleting the appropriate columns and/or tables from the database. We can define an analogous trigger realize_delete that does this.

These application of meta-functionality may seem somewhat perverse, but a distinct advantage is that table creation and deletion become inherently *relational* in nature (simple tuple insertions/deletions). Furthermore, this example highlights the uniform treatment of data and metadata in an MRDBMS in that metadata is just ordinary data with side-effects.

Schema Updates Updates on our schema relation need to be handled in a manner similar to insertions and deletes. However, here the question arises of what happens to the underlying data if a schema element is updated. If the update involves a simple name change (to either the relation pathname and/or the attribute), no further action is necessary since the underlying data remains the same.

The situation is more complicated when an update occurs that changes the pathname of a relation with respect to only a subset of the columns belonging to that relation. There are two ways we can approach this:

1. The update is treated as a delete followed by an insertion. In this case, the columns disappear from the original relation, and new (empty) columns are added to the new relation unless columns of the same name are pre-existing in that relation.
2. The update is treated as a restructuring operation where the old columns of data are moved into the new relation. In this case, a constraint must stipulate the order in which new values attach to old. This constraint can be formulated as an MCONSTRAINT in the original table declaration.

119

Promoting Data to Metadata As the previous paragraphs illustrate, a table with the meta-functionality of the schema table essentially allows the user to promote ordinary data to metadata. Note that values can be inserted into the table schema from other tables in the database, using a query in an INSERT statement. Thus, the user could simultaneously create multiple relation schemas (for example).

Furthermore, a limited form of the FIRA transpose operation (τ) can be obtained by allowing columns to be created from pre-existing data of the form in figure 1.

RDB::OldGrades

DB	Rel	Name	Assignment	Grade
SS	NewGrades	John	Asg1	78
SS	NewGrades	John	Asg2	73
SS	NewGrades	John	Asg3	88
SS	NewGrades	John	Asg4	82
SS	NewGrades	John	Asg5	84
SS	NewGrades	Jane	Asg1	50
SS	NewGrades	Jane	Asg2	53
SS	NewGrades	Jane	Asg3	48
SS	NewGrades	Jane	Asg5	67
SS	NewGrades	Spot	Asg1	90
SS	NewGrades	Spot	Asg2	85
SS	NewGrades	Spot	Asg3	96
SS	NewGrades	Spot	Asg4	89
SS	NewGrades	Spot	Asg5	98

(a)

```
INSERT INTO schema
    SELECT DB AS db_name,
        Rel AS rel_name,
        Assignment AS att_name,
        'Number' AS att_type,
        DATA(Grade GROUP BY Name)
    FROM RDB::OldGrades
```

(b)

SS::NewGrades

Name	Asg1	Asg2	Asg3	Asg4	Asg5
John	78	73	88	82	84
Jane	50	53	48	⊥	67
Spot	90	85	96	89	98

(c)

Fig. 1. MRDBMS "Transpose-Like" Transformation

The query in figure 1 (b) inserts tuples into the schema relation, with the side effect of creating the new relation SS::NewGrades shown in figure 1 (c). We have introduced a new function in the SELECT clause, DATA, which indicates where the data values that populate the new columns are to be obtained from. The novel use of a GROUP BY expression within the DATA function indicates how the values are to be partitioned into the new columns (in this example, the partitioning is based on matching Name values). Work is currently underway to formalize the semantics of the DATA function. In practice, there should also be constraints on the shape and contents of the originating relation (here, the relation RDB::OldGrades). These constraints can themselves be formulated within the MRDBMS framework.

Demoting Metadata to Data The data in a meta-relation can be appropriately termed *metadata*. As long as appropriate meta-functionality exists, the data in a meta-relation indeed captures the canonical notion of metadata as governing the schema of a federation. Given this, there are two natural ways to "demote" metadata to pure (non-functional) data:

1. Simply query the metadata directly (i.e. use the meta-relations "as is" in SQL queries). In the case of a dereference key (§2.3, below), however, access to the metadata itself may involve a DEFER command (see §2.3).

2. Drop all meta-functionality associated with a relation.

Usually, the first approach will be preferred. However, the second approach may be necessary if the order of meta-functional constraints becomes problematic due to the SQL:1999 definitions.

2.2 User-Defined Operational Constraints

Meta-relations can also come with constraints affecting the very nature of the relational querying operations, as illustrated in the following paragraphs.

Natural Joins The vast majority of equi-join operations are foreign key joins, but there may be more than one appropriate foreign key for a given relationship. In this case, a meta-relation join_hint can specify which foreign key is joined. Beyond this, join_hint can encode additional, user-defined constraints governing equi-joins.

```
CREATE TABLE join_hint AS
  ( col_ID1   NUMBER,
    col_ID2   NUMBER,
    PRIMARY KEY (col_ID1, col_ID2),
    FOREIGN KEY (col_ID1) REFERENCES schema,
    FOREIGN KEY (col_ID2) REFERENCES schema );
```

Simply put, a tuple appearing in relation join_hint means that the two columns indicated are joinable. Note that entries in this relation can be hand-coded individually, or can be inserted by an independent query. Thus, for example, we could stipulate that all columns of type "INTEGER" are joinable.

Currently, we would interpret join_hint as a set of *additional* indications to the usual pre-existing relational join constraints. However, in principle, the entire functionality of a natural join can be specified by a user of an MRDBMS using MASSERTIONs.

To capture this meta-functionality, we associate an MASSERTION with join_hint that specifies join_hint is to be checked whenever an appropriate equi-join arises.

```
CREATE MASSERTION joinable ( $R, $S)
   ON JOIN CHECK ( ( SELECT *
                     FROM join_hint )
                   CONTAINS
                   ( SELECT S1.col_ID, S2.col_ID
                     FROM schema S1, schema S2
                     WHERE S1.db_name::S1.rel_name = $R AND
                           S2.db_name::S2.rel_name = $S AND
                           S1.att_name = S2.att_name ) );
```

This example also highlights the need for an extended specification language for MASSERTIONs, beyond the SQL '99 facilities for ASSERTION declarations.

Aggregation In the case of aggregation, the aggregate functions are applied to columns of data. Again, the idea is that we can use a meta-relation to further restrict application of an aggregate function (or, ideally, to define the application in its entirety).

121

Dynamic Restructuring Along the same lines, we can specify when a particular column can be involved in a *relational transposition* operation, either as the result of data coercion such as arises from the DATA function (§2.1), or from the FIRA transpose operation, τ. Such a transformation involves promoting data to metadata and restructuring existing data appropriately. In the MRDBMS framework, we can specify when a particular column can be promoted to metadata. Thus, for example, we can avoid promoting real numbers to column headings.

Schema Independence A defining benefit of the MRDBMS framework is that user-defined constraints can be specified in a *schema independent* fashion. This means, for example, that the MASSERTION joinable will not have to be reformulated if the schema of the database changes. Similarly, as we will see below (§2.4) other external constraints can be formulated with schema independent code. This is an important benefit of allowing variables to be defined over relations in the meta-constraint language.

2.3 Schema Interoperation

In FISQL, one of the fundamental metadata accessing techniques is to *dereference* a column of values, tuple-by-tuple, as if they were attribute headings. This is reflected in the syntax "T.A.B" in FISQL, and the corresponding FIRA Δ operator [9]. A similar phenomenon can be achieved independently through the use of MCONSTRAINTs. In the schema table, for example, when a col_ID value is selected, *the values in the named column are referenced, rather than the ID value itself*. To achieve this, we define a new class of MCONSTRAINT, defining col_ID as a *dereference key*.

```
CREATE TABLE schema AS
       ( db_name   STRING NOT NULL,
         rel_name STRING NOT NULL,
         att_name STRING NOT NULL,
         att_type STRING NOT NULL,
         col_ID   AUTONUMBER,
         CONSTRAINT schema_pk PRIMARY KEY (col_ID),
         CONSTRAINT schema_ck UNIQUE (db_name, rel_name),

         /* new meta-constraint */
         MCONSTRAINT col_deref DEREFERENCE KEY
            FOR db_name::rel_name.att_name );
```

The MCONSTRAINT col_deref captures the idea that a col_ID is a place-holder for its associated column, and queries using the value col_ID in fact refer to fields in the named column. In other words, we want to use the data values appearing in the col_ID column of schema as if they were metadata (i.e. references to external data columns). This behavior can be side-stepped by *deferring* the col_deref constraint in the query. SQL:1999 already provides the capability to defer execution of constraints during a query.

As a canonical dereference example, suppose we want to determine all instances of the atom "John" in the database. We can do this with the following query:

122

```
SELECT  S.db_name, S.rel_name, S.att_name
FROM    schema S
WHERE   S.col_ID = 'John'; /* dereference col_ID */
```

The intended action of such a query is depicted in figure 2.

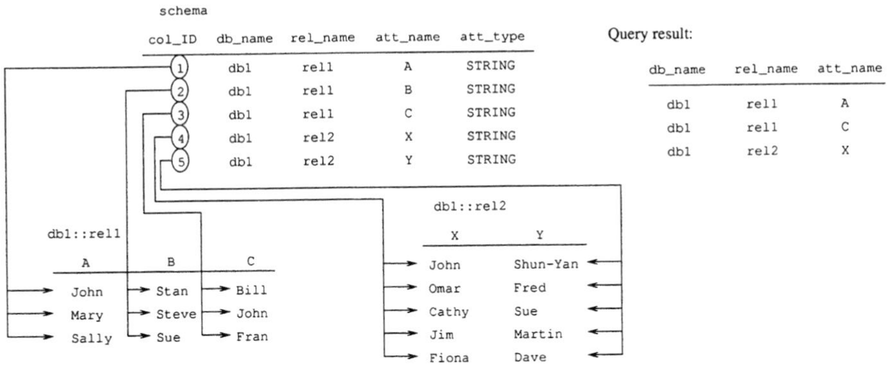

Fig. 2. Illustrating a dereference key

Relational Interoperability Note that the meta-functionality of a dereference key involves that a FROM clause definition such as FROM schema S may in fact be seen as ranging over all relations in the federation in the case where the col_ID attribute appears in the query. This imitates the behavior of the FIRA *generalized outer union* operator ($\sum$), which forms the outer union of all named relations in its argument. Previous sections have shown that we can also recapitulate the functionality of the FIRA transpose operator (τ). Thus, although our goal with MRDBMS was not to recapitulate the FISQL/FIRA framework, it is interesting that similar functionality emerges naturally within the MRDBMS framework. This is particularly significant in light of the *data/metadata transformational completeness* of the FISQL/FIRA framework.

2.4 Design Modeling

As another example of the applications of MRDBMS, consider the cardinality constraints arising within Entity-Relationship conceptual data models. For example, we might stipulate that a library user can borrow at most six books at any time. It is known that such constraints do not translate naturally into the relational model, but can be captured in SQL:1999 using constraints, assertions, and/or triggers. Thus, it is not surprising that such constraints can be captured within the MRDBMS framework, as it extends these facilities. What is new about the MRDBMS approach, is that a single meta-relation can encompass the cardinality constraints for *all* modeled relationships in the federation simultaneously. Thus, instead of writing and rewriting assertions governing particular relationships, we can create a single meta-relation, er_cardinalities governing all these cases. Furthermore, the assertions are formulated in a *schema independent* fashion, so that changes are not necessary when the underlying database schema changes. This is accomplished as follows.

```
CREATE TABLE er_cardinalities AS (
    entityDBName    STRING,
    entityRelName   STRING,
    relnshpDBName   STRING,
    relnshpRelName STRING,
    min_card    NUMBER,
    max_card    NUMBER
    MCONSTRAINT er_fk CHECK relnshpDBName::relnshpRelName
        HAS FOREIGN KEY FOR entityDBName::entityRelName);
```

The MCONSTRAINT included in the definition stipulates that the relationship table contains a (unique) foreign key for the entity table (this is the foreign key the min/max constraints will be checked against in the associated MASSERTION, below).

To capture the global meta-functionality of er_cardinalities, we define an associated MTRIGGER create_cardinality_constraints which in fact generates appropriate ordinary triggers, as follows. Thus, the user only need insert tuples in er_cardinalities to specify the min/max constraints of the design model.

```
CREATE MTRIGGER create_cardinality_constraints
    AFTER INSERT ON er_cardinalities AS
FOR EACH ROW
    fkey := er_fk(new.relnshpDBName::new.relnshpRelName);
    max := (SELECT max_card
            FROM er_cardinalities ERC
            WHERE ERC.relnshpDBName = new.relnshpDBName AND
                ERC.relnshpRelName = new.relnshpRelName);
    min := (SELECT min_card
            FROM er_cardinalitites ERC
            WHERE ERC.relnshpDBName = new.relnshpDBName AND
                ERC.relnshpRelName = new.relnshpDBName);
BEGIN
    CREATE TRIGGER :new.relationship|'_handle_constraints'
        AFTER INSERT ON new.relationship AS
    FOR EACH ROW
    BEGIN
        IF  ( (SELECT COUNT(fkey) + 1
                FROM new.relnshpDBName::new.relnshpRelName )
                    >  max ) THEN
            raise_application_error('Max constraint violated');
        IF  ( (SELECT COUNT(fkey) + 1
                FROM new.relnshpDBName::new.relnshpRelName )
                    < min ) THEN
            raise_application_error('Min constraint violated');
    END;
END;
```

The expression :x returns the actual symbolic value of x as a string, and | indicates string concatenation. Also, we assume the MCONSTRAINT er_fk can access the particular foreign key that the relationship uses to refer to the relevant entity relation.

3 Implementation Issues

A main concern when implementing MRDBMS functionality is efficiency. A prototype implementation "from the ground up" highlights the need for building from existing, optimized management systems due to efficiency and scalability concerns [1]. Interestingly, we can back-end an implementation of MRDBMS as above directly in existing platforms (such as Oracle), using PL/SQL and Oracle's string manipulation capabilities.

However, the MRDBMS architecture may benefit from being *invasive* in the sense that it reworks existing ASSERTION, CONSTRAINT, and TRIGGER implementations. Thus, beginning with an open-source database management system such as PostgreSQL [7] may prove fruitful until industry collaboration is attained. One advantage of this approach is that we can utilize novel file storage and access techniques such as *column files* [1] to facilitate schema updates.

Beyond this, it is known that a drawback to the database-driven constraint capabilities in existing database systems is that global constraints (TRIGGERS and/or ASSERTIONS) can be difficult to optimize and (if invoked frequently during ordinary transactions) computationally unfeasible. This gives reason to believe that the project of including intrinsic *database-driven* support for MRDBMS functionality may be untenable in practice. Balancing this is a general desire to include support for metadata querying and restructuring in FIS systems, since it is widely assumed such support must underlie truly automatic interoperation. An implementation of the MRDBMS functionality can provide insight into the types of metadata querying and restructuring that *can* be handled efficiently, and give some defining features of such cases, which could be written into the meta-CONSTRAINT language proposed in the previous sections.

4 Related and Ongoing Work

In this paper, we have presented examples of intrinsic, *database-driven* support for interoperability in relational federations. Our examples show that an extended meta-CONSTRAINT language can be provided which associates meta-functionality with relations. Relations with such functionality are then termed meta-relations.

Preceding approaches to data sharing frameworks almost without exception involve additional complexity in the data model [9]. A canonical approach is to utilize *complex objects* to store data (this is the approach taken by the TSIMMIS project, for example [3]). Although using complex objects incurs significant overhead in terms of both efficiency considerations and incompatibility with the relational model (by far the dominant data storage model in use today), it was previously thought that the relational model was insufficiently expressive to handle the needs of automatic data interoperation and restructuring [9]. Recently, it has been demonstrated that the relational model can indeed support sufficient and efficient restructuring, with simple and natural extensions [10, 11]. These extensions involve adding restructuring capabilities to SQL (obtaining a backward-compatible declarative language, *Federated Interoperable SQL*, or FISQL), and adding equivalent restructuring capabilities to the relational algebra (obtaining a powerful and efficient extended algebra, the *Federated Interoperable RA*, or FIRA).

The proposed work can be seen as a natural continuation of the idea of seamlessly manipulating both metadata and data in a relational setting that is exemplified by FISQL/FIRA [9]. FISQL/FIRA in turn arises out of pioneering work on SchemaSQL and SchemaLog [8], HiLog [4], and several other interoperability languages [9].

Work on active databases is ongoing [6], and the MTRIGGER construct would need to be investigated in this context. In particular, it seems likely the meta-functionality provided by MTRIGGERS would raise a host of issues of well-foundedness and efficiency, unless care is taken to restrict the meta-CONSTRAINT language appropriately.

Finally, we conclude with some idea of ongoing work. In MRDBMS as presented here, meta-functionality is attached to particular relations (and/or columns). This level of granularity may not be most appropriate. We are currently investigating the results of attaching meta-functionality to relational *datatypes*. This idea leads directly to parallels with self-describing data and (in particular) XML schemas.

In general, the goal of using data/metadata transformations in conjunction with mappings from XML data to relational data would be to use the metadata descriptions of the XML data as both metadata and data in the target relational system. This flexibility may support fully functional relational querying of XML native data, a goal which we are currently pursuing.

References

1. Mehdi M. Akhavein. *MetaSQL: A Database System with SQL Mutable Structure*. Master's Thesis, Emory University, November 2002.
2. Mehdi M. Akhavein, Shun Yan Cheung, James J. Lu, and Catharine M. Wyss. *Managing XML Schemas through XRDB*. IKE 2003.
3. Chawathe, S., Garcia-Molina, H., Hammer, J., Ireland, K., Papakonstantinou, Y., Ullman, J., and Widom, J., *The TSIMMIS project: integration of heterogeneous information sources*, IPSJ Conference, 1994.
4. Widong Chen, Michael Kifer, and David S. Warren. *HiLog: A Foundation for Higher-Order Logic Programming*. Technical Report, SUNY at Stony Brook, 1990.
5. Maurizio Lenzerini. *Data Integration: A Theoretical Perspective*. Invited tutorial, PODS 2002.
6. Norman W. Paton, D. Gries, and F. Schneider (eds). *Active Rules in Database Systems*. Springer-Verlag, December 1998.
7. *PostgreSQL*. http://www.postgresql.org
8. Narayana Iyer Subramanian. *A Foundation for Integrating Heterogeneous Data Sources*. Ph.D. Thesis, Concordia University, August 1997.
9. Catharine M. Wyss. *Relational Interoperability*. Ph.D. Dissertation, Indiana University at Bloomington, August 2002. http://www.fisql.com
10. Catharine M. Wyss, Felix I. Wyss, and Dirk Van Gucht. *Augmenting SQL with Dynamic Typing to Support Interoperability*. EFIS 2001.
11. Catharine M. Wyss and Dirk Van Gucht. *A Relational Algebra from Data/Metadata Integration in a Federated Database System*. CIKM 2001.